THE
LOVING
YOURSELF
BOOK FOR
WOMEN

A Practical Guide to Boost Self-Esteem, Heal Your
Inner Child and Celebrate the Woman You Are

DIANA RACHEL BLETTER

FOR MY SISTER, CYNTHIA,
THE GIRLS WE WERE AND THE WOMEN WE'VE BECOME;
FOR MY YOUNGER DAUGHTER, LIBBY,
WHO ENCOURAGED ME TO WRITE THIS BOOK;
AND TO EVERY WOMAN READING IT.

You can travel around the whole world,
but you'll never find anyone who deserves your love
as much as you.

CONTENTS

"How much we know and understand ourselves is critically important, but there is something that is even more essential to living a wholehearted life: loving ourselves." — Brené Brown

Introduction

Congratulations! If you're reading this book, that means you're ready to walk on a journey toward loving the woman you are. Using these practical tools to love yourself can help infuse your days with joy, boost your self-confidence, and increase your self-esteem.

Studies show that being kinder to ourselves is the key to greater happiness. And yet, so many women seem desperate to figure out how to do just that. We treat our pets far better than we treat ourselves. But learning to love ourselves is the most important work we must do in our lives, for out of self-love comes everything else: healthy relationships, a meaningful job, and a satisfying, fulfilling, and happy life.

Loving yourself means doing things each day to make you feel that love. In this book, I will show you how these tools can help you in all aspects of your life, no matter what you face—whether you're getting married or staying married, having children or applying for a new job—because self-love is the most effective way to live, make good choices, take action, and be content in your life.

Loving yourself will help you:

- Make appropriate choices
- Take care of yourself
- Boost your self-esteem
- Let go of expectations
- Lose your resentments
- Conquer fear
- Learn acceptance
- Heal your relationships

For years, I didn't know how to do any of the above. I had no idea how to love myself.

Growing up with two alcoholic parents, I could only guess at what it would feel like to be safe inside myself, content, and self-loving. Like many other women, I also experienced sexual abuse. That's not uncommon; the Centers for Disease Control and Prevention reports that more than half of women have experienced some kind of sexual violence involving physical contact in their lifetime as adults. One in four women experienced sexual abuse as little girls. I'm one of those little girls.

I could never get a handle on not feeling that it was somehow my fault. I was somehow dirty and bad, and this shame lingered like a shadow over my life. I pushed away the pain, but I also couldn't feel much joy. Inside, I was numb, and there was a big, bold, deep *X* slashed across my soul. That meant defective. That meant there was no room to love myself. Hating myself seemed natural to me.

We often think of post-traumatic stress disorder (PTSD) as a condition that impacts men, mostly soldiers returning from wars. But symptoms of PTSD, including depression and anxiety, also plague women who've experienced some kind of sexual trauma. In fact, the National Center for Health Statistics has found that twice as many American women than men take antidepressants. It seems that women are constantly searching for ways to feel better about themselves.

Our vulnerability and struggle to find our place in the world haunt many of us.

One afternoon, I attended the funeral of a very good friend who died from ovarian cancer. I was heartbroken because she'd died so young. It dawned on me that life is short, and it could end at any moment. Was I going to spend my whole life hating myself? But how would I ever feel self-esteem, let alone self-love?

It's been many years since I began my journey toward loving myself.

I found a therapist who suggested I join a self-help group, an important suggestion that helped me grow even further. In this support group, I found someone to guide me. In twelve-step groups, these guides are called sponsors. Sponsors are like life coaches, but they're never paid. They volunteer to pass on what they've learned for free. My sponsor's name was Maggie; she was a shining example of what it meant to be a woman who carried herself with self-esteem, grace, and dignity. She's since passed away, but she taught me so much about loving myself, protecting myself—and just being myself.

After a while, I became a sponsor for other women, passing on what Maggie and other women have taught me. I continue to help other women because I believe I can keep what I've learned only if I give it away.

I've come to understand that we each have a story to tell; we each have survived difficult experiences. We're heroes of our own life story. And there's much we can learn from one another. I've spent hundreds of hours listening to women talk about the steps they took to heal themselves and then to love themselves. I've worked like a scientist in a laboratory, applying other women's tips, tools, and suggestions to improve my own situation. Every day I did the work. Every day I still do the work. Learning to love myself isn't something that happens overnight. This is a daily practice because life itself is a daily practice. Slowly, I began to feel I could not only love the woman I am but celebrate who I am.

This book is a compilation of all that I've learned that I want to pass on to you.

By loving yourself, you'll be able to tap into a deep reservoir of healing and power. You'll see that you're never alone. You'll understand that it doesn't matter who abandons you, because you'll learn to never abandon yourself. You'll be able to face any problem or crisis in life with a solid inner core, feeling as if the sun is always shining down upon you and you're channeling all the love in the Universe.

How do you achieve self-love? What does it look like? What does it feel like? How do you manifest it on a daily basis?

Loving yourself is:

- The ability to say no to others and yes to yourself
- Practicing self-care
- Saying, "I'd rather do this" or "I'd rather not do that" instead of "I don't mind" or "I don't care"
- Treating yourself with tenderness, the way you treat your puppy, kitten, child, or loved one
- Standing in a crowd of people and not competing or comparing
- Feeling content being you, even when your life is difficult
- Filling your own well and not waiting for other people or outside things to fill it

By taking practical, concrete steps like these to love myself, I feel like I've escaped this murky darkness. My life has improved in ways that are better than I could have ever imagined. I've achieved some of the goals I once considered pipe dreams. I started my own business, wrote several books, and raised four children and two stepchildren. I used to think that all I could give my children was a legacy of sorrow and disappointment, but now I believe I gave them support, encouraging them to not only be themselves but to *love* themselves. Love that goes from ourselves and to ourselves: it's as simple as that.

This book is divided into ten chapters.

In chapters 1 and 2, you'll learn how to be calmer throughout the day by having a morning routine and connecting to your body, heart, mind, and soul. If you take care of these four elements, you'll feel an increasing sense of wholeness.

Chapters 3 through 8 will help you handle difficulties that we all face: how to boost self-esteem, let go of expectations, stop self-doubt, conquer fear, make decisions, and practice acceptance.

Chapter 9 will inspire you to investigate your family history and how it impacts you.

And Chapter 10 shows that once you've healed the relationship with yourself, you can heal your relationships with others.

Throughout the book, I've changed the names of the women I've spoken with, adding dramatized details to protect their anonymity.

Loving ourselves is the most crucial course in the School of Life. We never graduate learning how to do this. It's a practice we do each day. Once you've started the journey, I encourage you to continue it. If you need more help, you deserve to get it. You can find professionals to talk to, and you can join self-help groups that will continue to show you how to love yourself.

"To love oneself is the beginning of a lifelong romance."
— Oscar Wilde

The Loving-Yourself Vow
Whenever I work with a woman on loving herself, I ask her to hold a ceremony in which she makes a vow to do that. Because somewhere along the way, our connection to our inner selves was severed. We stopped paying attention to that little voice inside us,

that little girl inside us who's vulnerable, hurting, possibly scared, confused, and alone. So we need to repair that connection to that child we once were—the truest core of us—and strengthen it.

And just as people get married and vow their love for one another, it's crucial to vow your love for yourself. Before you read this book any further, please stop and take a few moments to confirm your commitment to love yourself out loud. At first you might feel silly—as many women, including myself, have said— but then, just hearing your own voice can give you a rush of love, as if you were channeling all the love of the Universe right into you. I'd never understood the idea that love for myself isn't performance-based. It's just love. And once I tapped into that, I felt power, resolve, and a bubbly sense of joy. I went from feeling that my cup was half empty, to my cup was half full, to my cup was overflowing.

So, prepare a nice environment for yourself. You can be inside a room you like, outside on a beach, or under your favorite tree. Set up a little altar with things that are special to you: shells, stones, pine cones, or acorns. You can light a candle, a sage stick, or incense. Put on some clothes that make you feel like your truest, best self. It could be a long, flowing robe, a pair of leggings, or a comfortable sweater. Make sure you have a mirror, ring, bracelet, necklace, or earrings on hand.

Then, look at yourself in the mirror and say a vow to love yourself.

Here are a few examples. The first is my own. I knew I had to not only love my adult self but find a way to love that little girl inside me, whom I'd neglected for so long.

"Deenie, [that is one of my childhood nicknames], I love you. I'm sorry you had to go through the things you went through. But you're safe with me now, and I'll never let anyone hurt you again. My love for you is endless. I am who I am because of your bravery and resilience. I promise to always love you. I promise to listen to you and to never ignore you. I promise to always be there for you from now on. Forever."

"_____ [your name, your childhood name or nickname, or whatever you call yourself], I promise to believe in your talent, support your dreams, and always listen to you. I'll be with you in sickness and health, in failure and triumph, in plenty and in want. I'm with you always, from now on."

"_____ [your name, your childhood name, or nickname, or whatever you call yourself], you know me better than anyone else. You know my strengths and my weaknesses. I promise to always be patient, forgiving, and kind to you. I promise to be your best friend, from now on and always."

Now, cross your arms over your chest and give yourself a hug. A really big hug.

Hold it for a while so you take in that swoosh of love for yourself. If you're also loving that little girl inside you, take her hand.

When you're ready, put on the piece of jewelry. That will serve as a reminder that you're embarking on this journey of self-love. I wear a ring my mother used to wear, and in times of stress, I can look down on it and feel her strength and love, however flawed and broken. The gift of love is something we each must do not only by ourselves but *with* ourselves and *for* ourselves.

Whichever vow you say, write it down and tape it to your mirror or carry it with you. That way, you can remember what you promised to do. There's no other love like the love you have for yourself. Armed with that, you can face anything life throws your way.

"What lies behind us and what lies before us are tiny matters compared to what lies within us." — Ralph Waldo Emerson

Self-Love Checklist

If you're going to start on the journey toward self-love, you need to start exactly where you are. So I'd like you to answer the following yes-or-no questions. By the end of this book, I'll ask you the same questions, and you'll be able to see the progress you've made. Please don't find your answers to this checklist as another reason to bully yourself. Instead, see them as a starting point from which you'll notice that you're progressing beautifully. You've begun the work, which is the best gift you can give yourself.

- Do you have a hidden fear that people won't like you when they find out who you really are?
- Do you secretly hate yourself?
- Do you live in a state of dissatisfaction with your life?
- Do you feel worthless?
- Do you find yourself always reacting to what other people say or do?
- Do you want to please people even at the risk of not pleasing yourself?
- Do you fear making decisions?
- Do you take care of other people's needs before you take care of your own?
- Do the people surrounding you disappoint you often?

- Do you need other people's approval?
- Do you feel hopeless?

If you answered *yes* to some—or many—of these questions, don't despair. I can relate to how you feel because at one time, I answered *yes* to all of them. I understand because I desperately needed other people's approval, and I felt worthless, hopeless, and full of self-hate. But don't give up on yourself. Keep reading this book. These practical—and doable—tools helped me, and countless other women, and I know they can help you, too.

CHAPTER ONE

Loving Yourself as a Daily Practice

"The absence of love in our lives is what makes them seem raw and unfinished." — Ingrid Bengis

---

It was New Year's Eve, and my parents were drinking too much. They thought it would be funny to let my one-year-old sister drink some of their champagne. I was three years old at the time. Afterward, they put her in her crib in our bedroom, and she fell out.

She started crying, and my parents, who were in the living room, came into our bedroom. I watched the scene, witnessing the panic and fright. My mother screamed at me for not watching her, then screamed at my father. In those few moments, I absorbed a number of lessons that stayed with me:

- I needed to watch out for others, and watch over them.
- I needed to be very good and very quiet and never cause any trouble.

- I needed to be hypervigilant because something bad could happen at any moment.
- I needed to focus on the needs of the people around me and forget about my own.

That moment has stayed in my memory, trailing me. It was the start of a pattern in the way I severed myself from my very core, so I no longer had connection to myself, because I was too concerned with everyone else. I intuitively sensed that chaos was just around the corner, and I had to be aware. I stopped loving myself, really, because there was no *me* to love. My whole focus became attending to my family around me and making sure we didn't fall over the edge into chaos. I sensed that something could go terribly wrong and it would somehow be my fault. I felt I had to be perfect in order to survive. I felt guilty for not being and doing more, and shame for being who I was.

I really thought I would go through my whole life numb in this way. When I was twelve, I wrote a poem, and the last lines were:

> *Yet I am afraid*
> *Afraid of the death that awaits me*
> *Not the quietness of slumber, for I have had a lifetime of*
> *sleeping, but rather, the hollowness of my grave*

I was hollowed out, sad, and empty. My mother smoked too much, drank too much, and cursed too much. She was overprotective when it came to my sister and me, but crass and rude with everyone else. When things seemed to be fine at home, she'd suddenly start fighting with my father, who would then walk out of the house, and we were never sure when—or if—he'd return. My sister had learning difficulties, which weren't diagnosed properly, and she struggled in school. It was especially painful for me because my mother often told me it was my fault my sister had problems. I was a very good student—"a tough act to follow." When I was sixteen, a cousin told me, "In your family, you were never taught basic things that we were taught," and then she never spoke to me again.

A Daily Practice

So how could I learn to love myself when there seemed nothing of value for me to love? I thought, *I really should learn to love myself.* And yet the entire concept seemed so far away and unattainable—something I'd never reach.

About the same time, I was thinking about becoming a vegetarian, and I asked a vegetarian friend, "How am I going to be a vegetarian for the rest of my life?"

"Take it a meal at a time," she said.

Before that moment, I thought I would figure out this whole how-to-love-myself business in a few weeks or months, at most, and then I'd get on with my life. I didn't realize that this *is* my life. Each and every day, I write my life story. Life is a necklace, a string of days, and each day is a diamond I can polish. If I view my life like this, then loving myself becomes a realistic goal, part of my daily routine. Rather than trying all at once to change everything, I can take small steps each day.

Gradually, I began to feel the love for myself spread inside me with warmth. And it's something I do every day.

I used to wake up in the morning with a groan. I hated when my alarm clock rang. I liked to sleep because it was safer than drugs or alcohol, easy to use, and had the same effect: oblivion. I didn't want to face the day. I didn't want to face myself.

It was crucial for me to go from saying, "Oh my God, it's morning again" to "Thank you, God, it's morning."

The first thing I used to do in the morning was turn on the television to watch bad news, open my telephone, check my email, then look at social media to see all the fabulous things everyone else seemed to be doing. It was like junk food, and very unhealthy.

Loving myself meant stopping all that. I stopped looking at what other people were doing and started focusing on my life and myself. I began charging my phone in another room; that way, I'm not tempted to peek, even for one instant.

We need to start our day by centering and calming ourselves. We need to be inside ourselves, to connect to ourselves. Having a ritual in the morning is a way to fill ourselves with serenity and start our day right.

When you open our eyes, as soon as you can, say some kind of prayer of thanks that you're alive for another day. I say, "Thank you, God, for giving me another day."

I use the term *God* above because it's only three letters for me to type. It's just a code word that I use so you immediately understand the spirit of what I'm talking about. But I'm not referring to a specific, traditional God. I'm not talking about a religious entity. Instead, I'm talking about a spiritual force that goes beyond the bounds of religions.

There's no one definition. Instead of the word *God*, you can use *Goddess, Creative Spirit, Creative Force, the Great Creator, Higher Force, Higher Power,* or *Divine Presence.* You can think of your own term, a word or two that speak to you; a name that connects you to this spiritual light. It's a way to tap into an invisible source of extra strength when you feel depleted. Then you can thank the Divine Presence, the Universe, or whatever you do believe in. The important piece to loving yourself is loving the fact that you've been created—you're alive and on Earth. The Universe worked billions of years just to create you!

True statements like this can get you centered and ready for the day. One of the benefits of loving yourself is that you give yourself permission to do whatever you think will make you feel good.

Women all over the world are writing their own prayers, and not only reciting the prayers they've been taught as children. This is powerful. We give ourselves authority to be spiritual beings who can reach out to the divine.

Here are some prayers that women have told me they use:

- God, I offer myself to you. Help me be the woman you called me to be.
- Thank you, Divine spirit, for creating me. You're love, and I'll channel your love throughout the day.
- Today I'll trust that I'm exactly where I'm supposed to be.

- Higher Power, help me to do everything I have to do today.

I started using my prayer when I'd hear one of my babies crying in the next room. Believe me, at four thirty in the morning, it was hard to find a lot of thanks. But I said it and then went about doing what I was supposed to do. It helped center me. I felt like I had the oomph of the Universe behind me.

Self-Reflection
What kind of prayer can you say to start your day?

Down and Dirty
We can practice self-love even in the bathroom. Especially in the bathroom, because it never gets more down and dirty than in there.

After I brush my teeth and wash my face, I pat my face dry with a towel.

What's so special about that? Well, I used to rub my skin dry as if I were swatting away a fly. I didn't think about it. Now, I do it lovingly, the way I used to pat my babies dry. I do it with care because I care about myself.

Even if we have children to take care of and absolutely no time to indulge in a bubble bath or even take a shower for more than two minutes, it's still important that we do this one little act of kindness for ourselves.

You can pat your faces with love. It's a simple, powerful act. It's a physical way to love yourself. You deserve to have your skin soothed and smoothed. You deserve to take care of yourself.

Then you can look in the mirror.

Yep. Mirror, mirror on the wall.

I always hated looking at myself in the mirror. When I was a teenager, I looked for pimples and blackheads; as I grew older, I looked for blotches and bumps and wrinkles that seem to leave their indelible lines overnight. I had a tendency to look for imperfections on my face the way I looked for imperfections everywhere.

But now I make it a practice to ignore everything else on my face and look in my own eyes, deep into my soul.

Then I have to say the three hardest words:

I LOVE YOU.

I say my name, Deenie. I say, "Baby, baby." I say, "Sweetie, I love you. My little klumpie, kungie, precious child, sweet girl, I love you."

"Iiiiiiiiiiii Lllllllooovveee Yoooouuuu!"

There. It took me so long to feel that love. It took so long to do this without getting disgusted. I thought it was so silly. Stupid, even. I didn't think it would work. I felt so uncomfortable. That was before I took a vow to love myself. Back then I wanted to throw a rock at my own reflection. Yet I kept at it because I wanted so much to dislodge that boulder of shame and self-hate inside me. Over time, I began to say it like I meant it.

When I worked as a secretary, a boss once yelled at me for doing something wrong. I absolutely hated how he spoke to me. I mumbled to myself, "I don't like to be talked to like that." But I needed the money. I held myself back from crying and then excused myself to go to the restroom. I checked under the stalls and made sure I was alone. Then I stood in front of the mirror and whispered those three little words that are so powerful.

"I love you."

I stood there another moment, gave myself a big hug, and whispered, "I'll never let that man hurt you." Suddenly, I felt as if the little girl inside me was giving me courage. Saying those words made me stand up straighter. In the past, I would have minimized his reaction and tried harder to please him. But this time, I left the restroom, finished my day, and never returned to that company.

When we love ourselves, it doesn't matter who doesn't love us. We can feel that love no matter what. Even if our boyfriend just broke up with us, our landlord just raised the rent, or we're pissed off and scared and confused. We find a mirror. We say to ourselves, "I love you. We'll get through this."

I didn't believe it at first. I used to think, *How can I tell myself I love myself when I feel so crappy?*

This is what I told myself: "Fake it until you make it." I had to act as if I believed I loved myself. For days on end, I felt like I was lying. I wanted to shatter the image reflected in the mirror into a zillion pieces. But I kept doing it, and it started to get easier.

At self-help groups, people often say, "The group loved me until I could learn to love myself." So, let me be the one to say that you are loveable. I love you like your best friend, like your older sister, your favorite aunt, your mother, or sweet grandmother who comes back into your life to shower you with love. I know that you're trying your best to live in this world. I'm telling you again that I'll keep loving you until you learn how to love yourself.

Self-Reflection

Can you look in the mirror and say those three difficult yet magic words, *I love you*? How do you feel when you say that to yourself?

Along with saying "I love you" to ourselves, we need to take care of ourselves. That means regular checkups at the doctor and the dentist. Keeping ourselves washed and in clean clothes. It means we no longer deprive ourselves of sleep or push ourselves to do more and more until we drop from exhaustion. Workhorses need their rest, and so do we. Horses need checkups to make sure their horseshoes fit properly and aren't worn down. We need the same kind of care and attention.

We're human beings, not human doings. We need to remember that.

Self-Reflection

Do you take care of your personal hygiene? Get regular checkups at the doctor? The dentist?

Making Your Bed

The famous writer Paolo Coelho, author of *The Alchemist*, wrote a list of important things people need to do in life. "Know your worth," he says. "Take chances. Make your bed."

Making your bed is a small act of kindness you can do for yourself.

When my kids were small, making my own bed was the last thing on my mind when I had to get them to school and me to work. Sometimes I just didn't have enough time to do it, and I'd come home and do it after work, even if I was going to get back into it in a few hours.

In hotels, there are people—more like magic elves—who come in and make the bed when guests aren't there. It's a way for hotels to spoil their guests and make them feel cozy and comfortable. That's what I try to do for myself—make myself feel cozy and comfortable. When we talk about loving ourselves, we mean doing little acts to show we care. We're treating ourselves right. Once again, even on days when you don't have the time, at least take thirty seconds—that's all it takes—to throw the blanket over your bed. It's a way to pamper yourself.

It's also an important discipline that sets the rhythm for your day. Did you know that one of the first things that's stressed in rehab centers is the importance of people making their own beds? Making our beds is like making our own minds work correctly. Keeping our things in order helps our minds keep us in order. I've learned that if I take this action of making my bed, I get a better foothold on my day.

Aristotle said, "What we learn to do, we learn by doing." I could see that if I really wanted to love myself, I had to do these little things to feel it.

Self-Reflection
What is your bed-making routine? What would you like to change?

Now, I'm going to say something that will make me blush.

Before I learned to love myself, I always had ripped, slightly stained underpants. I was married, but I didn't have nice underwear. I thought my first husband should love me not because of my underwear but despite it. It was like a challenge. I dared him to like me!

Then I started going to a therapist, whom I used to call Dr. Good Person because he was just that—a good person. He helped me chip away at the terrible feelings I had about myself. One day, I told him proudly, "I bought underwear for everyone in the family today."

"Everyone?" he asked.

"Yes, everyone." I was thinking of the underpants for each day of the week that I'd bought for my daughters, and the Spider-Man and Batman underwear I'd bought for my sons, plus the new underpants I'd found for my husband.

"EVERYONE IN YOUR FAMILY?" he asked.

I suddenly turned red as a tomato. I'd forgotten the most important person in my life! ME!

I hadn't put myself on my own shopping list. I'd been focused only on buying for my loved ones. I'd been so caught up in what my family needed that I'd ignored my own needs.

That was the start of putting myself on my own shopping list. I started a habit of making sure I have nice underwear. I'm not talking about lacy, frilly, alluring underwear, which is also super-duper, but everyday underwear that symbolizes my developing love for myself. And it isn't only because I want to make a good impression on the emergency responders who first reach me if I suddenly have to be rushed to the hospital. It's because I want to feel like I deserve it.

One of the most important principles I've learned in years of working with myself and other women is this:

The amount of love we have for ourselves is equal to the state of our underwear.

And while we're on the subject, what does your underwear drawer look like? Mine used to look like blotches of paint. Everything was in bunches. As part of learning to love myself, I've learned to take care of my things. My underwear drawer began to come first. I realized that I'd taken extra seconds to fold everyone else's underwear and never made enough time to fold my own.

Self-Reflection
What is the state of your underwear? What does your underwear drawer look like?

Suiting Up and Showing Up

Even if I'm in a hurry, I still try to put on my clothes in a loving way—the way I used to dress my children. I tie my shoes with care. I dress appropriately for each occasion. Some days we can wear dangling earrings and leopard boots and colorful stockings; on other days, we need to dress more conservatively for work. Yes, every day is sort of like Halloween. We have to dress up to play our part. That's a part of life. We suit up and show up for our life.

Self-Reflection

What's your attitude toward your clothes? What can you change or improve?

"Give every day the chance to become the most beautiful day of your life." — Mark Twain

When my children were small and playing a game, they used to yell, "Do over!"

We don't get a do-over in life, but we can think of life as a whole necklace of well-lived days. We start with the morning and then continue, checking in with ourselves throughout the day. The past unfurls behind us, and the future isn't here yet. If you view your life as a necklace of diamonds, you can find a way to polish those diamonds. You can live more fully if you're focused on today.

And we can all remember that today is always the best day. It's the best day because it's the only day we have. The past is passed, and the future isn't here yet. We can focus on today, be in today, and do what we can to love ourselves.

Journaling

Keeping a journal is also a way to connect to yourself. I write it in my journal when I'm struggling to figure out what I'm feeling. Some women write a certain number of pages each morning as a discipline. Others write down their dreams or what they can do to prepare for the hours ahead.

There are no rules for writing in our journals. There are no rules for what kind of journal to have. I use unlined notebooks and write with a medium-tip pen because I like the feel of the ink flowing onto the page. I write in my journal every few days. For me, it isn't a memoir. In fact, every year, I browse my journal and then throw it in the recycling bin. I'm writing for my eyes alone, not for posterity. It's where I dump all my negative emotions, getting them out onto the page so that I don't inflict them on those I love. After I've written out my feelings, I often talk things over with someone else. Seeing my words on paper gives me a clearer sense of what's going on inside me.

When I'm struggling to accept a situation, I write a letter to God. A lot of women do this. Better yet, we can write a letter to God and then write a letter back from God.

Yes, you can be God's ghostwriter. You can channel God and write down everything you think God would say to you.

I started this practice when my stepson was diagnosed with cancer. I couldn't imagine how God could ever defend himself for giving cancer to this vibrant boy. But after a while, I found God writing these words: "I'm not taking your child. I'm receiving him." Somehow, that sentence comforted me and made me feel like God really was on my side. I felt a sense of peace growing inside me. My stepson did recover, and I found a lot of hope and comfort using this tool.

One woman I know, Brett, works in the movie business, so when she wrote a letter to God, she pictured God sitting in a Hollywood office, barking to his secretary, "Get me this woman's file!"

The secretary came back with the woman's file, and God opened it and wrote, "You won't believe all the good things I found in your file that I have planned for you! But you just have to wait a little bit longer while I sort things out. It took me millions of years just to get starlight down to earth, so give me a little time!"

That made Brett laugh. It brought her patience—and more acceptance.

Self-Reflection

Do you have a journal? Are you willing to start writing in one? Can you try writing a letter to God and asking God to write back?

A Word A Day

Another tool I've found is picking a word to focus on each day. There are so many awesome words to choose from:

- Intuitive

- Spark
- Connected
- Inspired
- Power
- Aware

A word a day helps me stay aware, connected, inspired, powerful, and sparked with desire to do my day right, full of self-love that brims over and touches other people—the strangers I happen to meet and my loved ones. A friend picks a word for the year and then tries to do things in line with that word. One year, she picked *muse*, and that included starting to paint and going to museums. It also included finding ways to a*muse* herself, picking activities she really enjoyed.

Self-Reflection
Do you want to pick a word a day? A word for each year?

Check In
Throughout the day, I stop and check in with myself. Did something just happen that's upsetting me? What can I do about it?

Our feelings come and go. Most of the time, we feel the feeling and let it pass. If the discomfort lingers, we can take a moment to find out why we're feeling it. Is it triggering an old fear? A childhood hurt? Remember, if the feeling seems hysterical, it's often historical. It's often a layer of a very old emotion from childhood, or perhaps, something you've stored inside from your family's past. It's important to explore your feelings. You can work with a therapist or in a support group to uncover hidden emotions so they don't run—or ruin—your life.

I try to not beat myself up if I don't do it perfectly. Some days we might feel full of self-love, and on other days, our inner tank seems like it's running on empty. If we're taking care of family members—either a little one or an elderly parent—it's difficult to find the time. But caretakers need to be taken care of too. I try to find a way to carve out a space for myself, even if it's only a few minutes. Even if it's just in the bathroom, where I can close the door, close my eyes, and breathe in deep.

Self-Reflection
Can you try to check in with yourself during the day? Do you notice anything different? Is there an improvement in your attitude?

We can take our Higher Power with us throughout the day, wherever we go. We are never alone.

At Night
Beating myself up, wishing I didn't say this, wondering why I didn't say that ... My demand for perfection from myself often makes me feel like a failure. So, before I go to sleep, I try to list three things I'm proud of myself about. Three things I said or

didn't say, did or didn't do. This is important. Loving myself means finding the little things I like about myself.

- I like the way I was quiet and listened when my husband disagreed with the way I handled that situation.
- I like how I didn't procrastinate and started working on my tax returns.
- I like that I went to the gym this morning for twenty minutes.

This is a powerful practice. It gives me concrete reasons to feel good about myself. It's like when I started falling in love and would tell my then future husband, "I like the way you smell. I like the curve of your shoulders." So, I try to find these things I like about myself each night before I go to sleep.

I also think of three things I have to be grateful for.

- I have warm socks and my toes aren't cold.
- I can move my arms and scratch my back where it itches.
- I ate a healthy dinner.

Filling my heart with thanks and not taking things for granted pumps me up with gratitude. Over time, by following these steps, I've gone from feeling my cup is half empty to feeling my cup is half full to feeling, now, that my cup is overflowing.

So, as you lay your head on your pillow and think of all these things you like about yourself, all these things you have to be grateful for, you may find yourself drifting off to the most pleasant, wonderfully, cozy, self-loving sleep.

And you can start the routine all over again tomorrow.

Self-Reflection

Can you think of three things you do during the day that you feel good about? And three things you have to be grateful for?

CHAPTER TWO

Taking Care of Ourselves

Each day is a room that you have never entered before.

I went through the motions of being an adult. I had a degree from a prestigious university, but I was living in a rundown studio apartment in a big city—just me and a thousand cockroaches—and working as a secretary for a temp agency. Every morning, the agency sent me somewhere else to substitute for another secretary. I was an anonymous worker whose name nobody could remember.

I was erasing myself.

And I hated it. Yet I didn't want to look for another job, a serious job, because I was scared I wouldn't get one. I didn't want to compete for a real job. I was so scared. I'd grown up thinking I had to be number one. Otherwise, I'd be a failure. It was all or nothing for me. So I'd dropped out and took work like a joke. My friends had moved on to grad school or law school, and soon I stopped working at the temp agency and began working as a waitress in a hamburger restaurant. Taxis and cars whizzed by, everyone with a place to go, but I felt stuck in my life.

I was unable to define myself and fell into a gaping hole of depression. I developed pains in my back that wouldn't go away. Eventually, I went to a Chinese acupuncturist.

I lay down on a narrow cot in his tiny room, which smelled like mushrooms and spices I couldn't name. There were bottles and boxes stacked on shelves that ran up and down the walls. I could hear the shouts and sounds of the street below the window. He poked me with needles. I was turning my body, my back—indeed, my entire life—over to this stranger who barely spoke English.

"I know what your problem is," he told me.

"Really?" I said, thinking it was curvature of the spine or a broken bone. Something I could easily fix so I could be on my way.

"Emotions wobbly!" he announced.

He was right. My emotions were wobbly and wound up. I realized then that my physical pain was a symptom of a deep emotional pain I'd been trying to avoid.

I wish I could remember that acupuncturist's name so I could thank him for launching me on a voyage of self-discovery. Soon after that, I found a therapist I could work with. I was finally able to understand that the most exciting, adventurous, and fascinating journeys begin within ourselves.

We set out with our internal compass to guide us. We make sure to take care of the four elements inside us: body, soul, heart, and mind. It doesn't matter in which order we choose to care for them, but we must take care of them.

Mind

I have to take care of my mind first because the first thing that starts awakening is my conscious awareness. I open my eyes. My mind is intact. My brain is functioning. When I think about people I know who suffer from dementia, I know how important it is for my mind to be operational.

And my mind is like a muscle. If I don't use it, I lose it. At some point during my day, I remember to read something that takes effort. I try to read an inspiring quote to get me motivated for the day.

The fact that you're reading this book is a sign that you've decided to take action. You get a standing ovation. Bravo!

Heart

I was feeling really depressed and empty inside. I was walking around, thinking about the time my mother accused me of wearing my new white lace ankle socks when I was actually wearing an old pair. She started spanking me all over and telling me I was a liar. Her words hurt more than her hits.

As I was walking and thinking about that spanking, I passed a toy store. I stopped, turned around, and went inside.

"What are you looking for?" the saleswoman asked me.

"I'm looking for a stuffed animal for a little girl," I replied.

I didn't tell her *I* was that little girl. I felt the little girl inside me needed some comforting. I walked up and down the aisles, looking at all the different stuffed animals. What would cheer me up? A giraffe? A teddy bear? A furry dog?

I chose a little bunny rabbit that plays a lullaby when I wind it up. That bunny rabbit is now more than twenty-five years old. When I get up in the morning and make my bed, I also tuck in that bunny. I have a big family with lots of people to love in my life, but that bunny symbolizes how I've found love for myself.

Sometimes I even feel love for the ordinary objects in my room. "Good morning, dresser," I say. "Good morning, lamp. Good morning, slippers." It's good karma, indeed, to appreciate everything in my life, including my ordinary things.

Self-Reflection

Do you have a comforting stuffed animal? What can you do to fill your heart?

Soul

The soul is invisible, yet so strong. People who have experienced death up-close can testify that even the smallest person is heavy once they've passed away. Some mystics believe it's because the soul is gone, and it's the soul that lifts the body.

There's no proof that the soul exists. And yet, we feel it. I feel it when I'm praying and the ancient words pour over my soul like soothing waters. The soul is a pure, celestial creation that's in tune with the heartbeat of the Universe. To thrive, our souls need prayer, meditation, quiet, tenderness, love, healing, and stardust.

Yes, stardust, because the soul is connected to the magical cosmos and all its mysteries.

You have to fill your own inner well, which is your soul. It's pure and it's good and it's invincible.

As the poet William Ernest Henley wrote, "I thank whatever gods may be/for my unconquerable soul."

My soul now feels unconquerable, but for the longest time, I felt a jagged X slashed across it. On the outside, I was a super achiever, someone who appeared to have everything. But the X meant I was an imposter. *If people really knew me*, I'd think, *they'd realize that I'm bad, fake, worthless.*

When I told my sponsor, Maggie, about how that X made me feel like a piece of shit, she said to me, "That's okay. I often feel like a big pile of shit."

"You feel like a big *pile* of shit?" I asked her. "You're so lucky! I only feel like a piece!"

A piece of shit. That was the X on my soul. I had to pour enough love over that X to bury it. I had to flood it with self-love so it got lost in the ocean. I had to treat myself with so much tenderness and kindness that the X shriveled and withered away. I had to fight against that self-hatred with a cavalry of self-loving thoughts that stampeded over it. In my soul, it was the battle of love versus hate, and love won out.

Love always does. It's stronger than hate. Our souls feel this love as the vibration of the Universe.

Prayer is a way to connect the soul to the higher forces in the Universe. I resisted this idea for some time because I didn't think some kind of presence "out there" could help me love myself.

But it did.

And the great thing about prayers is that each of us can choose our own. It doesn't matter which donkey we ride to get up the mountain as long as we keep ascending.

There's a beautiful story about a little girl who's holding a prayer book, but all she's doing is reciting the alphabet.

"What are you doing?" her mother asked. "You can't read."

"I know, but God understands my A B C."

When I was in high school, I used to visit the various churches in my town. My soul hungered for comfort. These days, I say traditional prayers from my childhood house of worship. I also say prayers that I make up, prayers in which I talk to God.

Self-Reflection

Do you have a prayer routine? Do you attend a house of worship? What can you do to improve your spiritual life through prayer?

Nina is a biotechnology scientist in her forties who never trusted anything that couldn't be proven. When she first talked to me, she was very skeptical about the notion of God. Then she began thinking about quantum physics, which she was familiar with, and it dawned on her that there *are* forces that exist but can't be seen. This helped her develop an idea of some kind of Higher Force. She now says that developing spirituality has been one of the most important benefits of loving herself. Feeling that she isn't alone, that she has some kind of power greater than herself to turn to, has helped her through crises.

If I forget my soul in the race for success, then I'll crash, burn, and lose everything anyway. If I forget my soul, I forget my purpose. I feel a buzz of discontentment. I need to keep my soul plugged into my Higher Power. I do this by filling my soul with gratitude and hope and replenishment. Some days, this might take only a few minutes. Other days, I need more time. Here are some things I do to nurture my soul:

- I listen to beautiful music, like Sarah Brightman singing "Dust in the Wind."
- I dance to this song or another one so my soul can take in the music. Then my whole body becomes a prayer.
- I go out in nature. I take a walk in a park and try to notice the beauty all around me: A spider's web. A worm. A bird soaring up into the endless sky. I can connect to my soul in nature because I am part of creation.

One day, I was walking in the woods, and I thought, *Look at all this beauty! Look at God's handiwork!* And then I had an even more powerful thought: *I'm part of God's artwork! I'm part of God's creation.*

We're now here on Earth—a part of the handiwork of the Universe right here, right now.

Self-Reflection

Where do you feel a connection to your Higher Power? What are some activities you can do?

To fill our souls, we must connect to that Higher Force who guides us. Prayer is talking to God, and meditation is listening. People had been telling me to meditate for years. I would sit down and get comfortable, and as soon as I closed my eyes, my brain was off, racing in a hundred directions. *Bam, bam, bam,* like a pinball machine, buzzing and blinking. I did it once or twice, wanted instant results, and when I didn't get them, I quit.

People who meditate say it's a valuable practice that invites serenity and love into their being. Quieting our minds is a skill that leads to spiritual growth. So I decided to try it again. I found a talk on meditation by a woman named Lorna. You can find the link to her talk in the reference section of this book. She was British with a quick wit, and she shared a simple sentence that never fails to comfort me. During her guided meditation, Lorna said, "God said, 'I am closer to you than the breath in your nostrils.'"

I tweaked Lorna's suggestion to encourage listeners to pay attention to their breathing to quiet their mind. I decided to repeat a mantra because I found I needed something to focus on. So when I breathe in, I say, "Trust God." When I breathe out, I say, "Let go." Sometimes, after I say, "Trust God," I hear a little voice that says, "I'm right here with you."

Wow.

Sometimes I'm able to get to that place where my mind really is blank and still and peaceful, and I see an orange-purple swath of peace on the backs of my eyelids. I'm not worrying or thinking about anything else, and I'm just in the moment. It's a state of being. It's almost bliss. That doesn't happen each time I meditate, but I still try to incorporate this practice into my day.

Don't be dismayed if your mind goes off to hum a tune, think about buying pillowcases, ponder what your child's teacher said, or decide what you want to make for dinner. After all, we think an average of fifty thoughts per minute. That's almost one every second.

This is an example of what my mind still does when I'm trying to meditate:

BREATHE IN.
Why does he keep saying that? It is so annoying!
BREATHE OUT.
I need to buy celery and parsley.
BREATHE IN.
Where did I put my boots?
BREATHE OUT.
I should cancel that subscription ...

Our minds are *supposed* to work hard because that's their job. But we need to learn to turn them off just to feel peaceful. Every time a thought pops into my brain, I just observe it (while trying not to judge it) and go back to concentrating on my breathing.

Let's go back to the example of what my meditation sometimes looks like. When I get started, my mind acts like a viral TikTok account, bouncing from thought to thought, frenetic and full of activity. Then I tell my mind to quiet down. Who is it that's giving direction to my mind? That's the true voice of my being. It isn't my mind. It's my soul's spokeswoman. The voice that commands my brain to grow quiet is my truest essence. It's the invisible spark in my soul. It's the place where I go to connect to my most loveable self. It's my home.

So, if I can reach that place and connect to it on a daily basis, I'm able to quiet my mind and tap into my soul. And my soul is part of God's handiwork. My soul is part of creation.

When I started, I'd meditate for three minutes. That was about as long as I could sit without getting restless. Then I'd meditate for five minutes. These days, I set my egg timer for twenty minutes and just sit in awareness. I don't use the alarm on the phone because the moment it rings, I have to move my hand to shut it off. I prefer to slowly come back from that place of peace.

Self-Reflection

Do you understand the connection between self-love and meditation? Have you tried meditation? Are you willing to try meditating seriously?

Body

My body is the temple that houses my heart, soul, and mind, so I take care of it as best as I can. Each day, I try to do some kind of exercise to stretch my body.

If I have only five minutes, I run in place or do a quick yoga routine. If I don't have time for that, I walk someplace instead of driving, or I use the stairs instead of taking an elevator. If I have three minutes, I can put on one song and dance.

For several years, I took a self-defense course. This helped me feel that I could try to protect myself from an attack. I couldn't go against a world-class fighter, but I now feel stronger. I like the idea that I have some basic self-defense skills.

When I lived in Kansas, couldn't afford to join a gym, and it was too cold and windy, I walked around a nearby mall in the early hours before the stores all opened. In warm weather, I love to swim and ride a bicycle. Exercise stretches my physical muscles and helps me feel alive and present.

And while we're talking about loving our bodies, let's talk a bit about food. Here are my Ten Food Commandments:

1. I'll try to stick to food with natural colors, like sweet potatoes, carrots, and apples. I try to avoid white food except for (my mouth is already watering) baked potatoes, baguettes, and vanilla ice cream.

2. I'll eat a lot of vegetables and won't listen to people who say fruit has too much sugar. Fruit has just the right amount of sugar my body needs.

3. I won't eat too late at night or right before I go to bed. I'll make sure my body is active when I'm eating so it has time to digest.

4. I won't deprive myself. I won't starve myself to reach an ideal weight that I can't maintain and isn't good for me anyway.

5. I won't eat food that I know I can't stop eating. My friend Mary Pat is addicted to sugar. Once she takes that first bite out of a doughnut, she's eating a dozen. She once

dove into a dumpster behind Dunkin' Donuts to find thrown-away doughnuts. Like an alcoholic who can't stop after the first drink, she can't stop after something sugary. Which is why I can't eat red licorice. Once I have a Twizzler, I'm devouring the whole package.

6. I don't sit down with a party-size bag of Cheetos. I fill one bowl to control the size of my portions. (I used this tip with my children, too, when they were small.)

7. I'll try not to eat a lot of food with a lot of artificial ingredients I can't even pronounce. If I can't say it, I won't eat it. True confession: I make exceptions for mocha chip ice cream and peanut M&Ms.

8. I won't drink soda except for an occasional natural ginger ale. That includes sugar-free soda.

9. I'll drink lots of water.

10. I'll try to make my meals rather than buy them. Home-cooked food has less salt and sugar, and I know what's going into my dish.

An important component to loving myself is getting to know myself and what's good for my body. When I'm more aware, I can figure out what's best for me. We can experiment with foods that feel right and those that don't. That's loving.

Oh, and I try to eat slower. People who eat slowly eat less. I have good table manners. I use a proper fork and knife unless I'm eating with chopsticks or having food from Ethiopia or another country where people use their fingers. I don't lick my plate. I don't smell or sniff my food before I eat it in public. At a restaurant, I place my used napkin by my plate and my silverware neatly across the plate. If I'm in a fast-food restaurant, I make sure to remove my tray and throw things out.

Over the years, Maggie and other women I've admired have encouraged me to try to take care of my heart, body, mind, and soul even if I have only ten minutes during the day. I used to ask, "How is ten minutes going to help me boost my self-esteem?" I didn't think it was possible. And yet, those ten minutes reverberate inside me, filling me with tenderness. Slowly, as I've grown in love for myself, I've become able to carry myself with grace and dignity.

Yet I felt far from graceful and dignified for most of my life. I didn't know how to treat myself nicely or take care of myself; I couldn't even concentrate long enough to make a schedule for my day. I thought a schedule was confining; it made me feel trapped. Yet I've come to understand that making a rough outline of the day helps me stay focused on my goals. I like to know what I'm doing so I can eagerly anticipate events during the day; I also like to mentally prepare for things I'm wary of. I can now move through my day with ease.

This wasn't so for Melissa, a straightforward, hard-working woman whose husband cheated on her and then moved out of the house. Melissa was devastated. She'd always imagined that her dinner table would always have her, her husband, and their two sons sitting around it. But life suddenly threw her a curveball and hit her in the face, the way life often does. For a while, she was so depressed that she took sick leave from work and spent her days in bed—in her pajamas, unwashed, and grungy. She had to start learning how to take care of herself from ground zero. When I'd ask her what she could do for herself each day, she had no idea.

I suggested she use the fifteen-minute tool. This tool is a lifesaver in crises, when we feel like we aren't able to function.

Melissa and I made a daily schedule that was broken down into fifteen-minute increments. This sounds crazy and controlling, but it's like doing an exercise routine where your coach blows a whistle every few minutes, and you have to go to the next exercise.

Melissa wrote down exactly what she was going to do each day, including taking a shower and picking out her clothes. Following the schedule gave her less time to obsess about her ex-husband and what the family dinner table would be like without her children's father—and with that empty chair. She even allowed herself a fifteen-minute slot on her schedule to sit at the table and look at the chair so she could mourn the end of her marriage.

It's been five years since Melissa's husband left. Of course, she's had some rough days, but she doesn't need the fifteen-minute tool anymore. Her kids have learned to survive the divorce, and so has she. Melissa has a new boyfriend with a cabin on a lake, where she's learned she likes fishing, something she never did with her ex-husband. She never even knew she liked it.

The fifteen-minute schedule becomes a ninja challenge. When we follow it, we become too preoccupied to stew, and we start to feel a bit better at the end of the day because we stuck to the schedule. Having a schedule doesn't make our pain go away, but it does help us get through a crisis.

Plus, on good days, having a schedule helps us take care of ourselves.

No matter how long you've lived, it's never too late to learn how to live.

Self-Reflection
Do you try to make a schedule for yourself each day? Can you improve it? How do you manage your time better during a crisis?

CHAPTER THREE

Boosting Self-Esteem

"Pain is the root of knowledge."
— Simone Weil

The pediatrician was a prominent man in town. Everyone respected him. Everyone except me. I used to cry before my mother took me to see him—and afterward. She thought it was because I got shots that hurt, but that wasn't the reason. Once I was in the exam room, he'd tell the nurse to leave. He'd tell my mother not to come into the room. He'd tell me to lie down on the examining table, completely naked. Then he'd rub my breasts and insert his finger into my vagina, saying he had to "check down there."

I told my mother, and she sort of believed me, but it was before #MeToo, before people talked about sexual abuse, before little girls ever spoke up against an authority figure. I didn't speak up about the doctor and his hands and his eyes and the way he leaned into the table and stood over me. And how he touched me, burning me up.

I still ignite with shame when I think about that. And rage. Anger doesn't even come close. The man is gone, and there's nothing I can do except tell the little girl I once was that I'll defend her to the best of my ability and will never, ever let anyone hurt her like that again.

The doctor's abuse robbed me of self-esteem. It made me feel like I had no say over what was happening to me. I wasn't in control of my body. I had no rights. I became an object for someone else, existing to meet the needs of others. I knew that what the doctor was doing didn't feel right, and it made me feel creepy and bad. But I was a little girl and couldn't stop him. And maybe there was something wrong about me that made him touch me like that.

As I wrote in my poem from long ago:

> *I have no life*
> *My breath is cut short of loving. My lips feel no kisses; my*
> *body feels no sweet caresses.*
> *Yet I am afraid …*

I lost myself then—another piece of me. I erased myself. I went numb. How could I feel self-esteem when I didn't have a self?

While I was writing this book, I looked in my old copy of the unabridged *The Random House Dictionary of the English Language* from 1966, which is a mere 2,059 pages. It defines *esteem* as: "to regard highly or favorably; regard with respect or admiration."

It has taken me hundreds of days to rebuild my self-esteem, and there are still moments when I feel shattered and cracked in pieces. Yet I try each day to set goals to boost my sense of wholeness and self-worth. These goals must be manageable because, as a friend who's a professor in statistics told me, "If the gap between what you want and what you can get is too wide, then you will probably give up."

"Let me first be sure what I intend and the reasons for my choice; this will guide my thoughts into constructive channels, and keep me from attempting the impractical or impossible." — Celebra Tueli

Our goals need to be realistic in terms of time, energy, and resources. This way, we'll keep trying and not quit. We can take our dreams seriously and go after them, but we also need to keep them tethered to reality so we don't get overwhelmed and frustrated. It's admirable to go after goals, but things don't always go the way we want them to. And that's when we have to work hard to accept life just as it is.

Almost two thousand years ago, Epictetus wrote, "What you have may seem small; you desire so much more." But, he suggested, "Let your desire go; covet not too much."

You may find that the best way to tackle a large project is to break it down into small, manageable parts. You can get out a pen and paper, a phone, or a tablet, and jot down all the things you need to do to reach your goal.

For example, when I wanted to get a new job, I had to write down everything I'd have to do:

- Update my résumé
- Contact friends
- Ask coworkers or my former employer if they'll be willing to be a reference
- Check job listings on four sites every day
- Send out résumés
- Go on interviews
- Get a haircut for interviews
- Have an outfit ready

When I did one thing on the list, I could check it off and feel like I'd accomplished something. Doing just one item gave me the self-esteem energy to go on to the next. However, I often felt overwhelmed before I even began. Updating my résumé, for example, seemed so daunting that I broke it down into even smaller segments.

- Just look at my résumé
- Go over it
- Maybe take notes

I checked off those three items, and I felt better already. This positive act boosted my self-esteem.

Start from Where You Are

> *"The secret to getting ahead is getting started."*
> — Mark Twain

I need to start exactly where I am. I need to bloom where I'm planted, which means that where I am is where I must begin.

After the birth of my first child, I was out of shape and weighed more than I wanted to. I knew that the best way for me to lose weight was to do aerobic exercise, so I decided to run. Whenever I could, I tied up my running shoes (with tenderness) and set out, huffing along, struggling to move my body. I knew I had a lot of work ahead of me, but I also knew I had to start from somewhere to boost my self-esteem. Just getting out there each morning made me feel good about myself.

Lack of self-esteem is partly due to the fact that we're often angry about where we are in life. Angry about how many miles we have yet to run. How far we need to go. If we're perfectionists, we get mad that we're not as perfect as we want to be. We beat ourselves up.

We sometimes spend too much time waiting and wishing and wanting things to be different. Before I started to run, I was angry that I'd never get into shape to run a marathon. I'd set my sights too high. I wanted to build my self-esteem, but I was unwilling to do anything about it. And I knew I had only two options:

Do nothing or do *something*.

The moment you decide to do something, you strengthen your self-esteem. I'll probably never run a marathon, and that's okay. I can accept where I am and do what I can.

The moment we take action, we begin to feel better. And we can't let the fear of failure stop us from trying

There's a story about a woman who wanted to play piano. She was forty-seven. She said to her piano teacher, "Do you know how old I'll be by the time I learn to play piano?"

"The same age you'll be if you don't," he replied.

Meaning, we get older anyway. The woman might not become a concert pianist, but she learned how to play. She didn't miss out on something just because she feared it wouldn't work out exactly the way she would have wanted it. Don't let your fear of failure, or your fear of not being as good as you'd like, stop you from trying. Just making the effort will boost your self-esteem.

If you want to learn how to speak Portuguese, let's say, don't get overwhelmed. Decide how long you want to study. For instance, you can set your timer for thirty minutes and study. Or you can decide to take just one lesson. After one lesson, you'll know more Portuguese than you knew before.

We can boost our self-esteem by asking ourselves what we want to do. So just start doing what you want to do. Do you want to learn how to bake sourdough bread? Play pickleball? Learn how to crochet?

This is a big deal for so many of us. I was always so tuned in to what other people wanted from me, that I went along with their desires. It's so wonderful to now ask myself what I want. Over the years, I've learned how to snowboard, make chocolate pudding from scratch, and tie-dye clothes. I don't do any of these things perfectly, but I enjoy them.

Anything worth doing is worth doing badly. We can hug ourselves for trying new things.

Self-Reflection

What are three things you want to try to do?

Getting a Commitment Buddy

We show up for ourselves and boost our self-esteem when we set out to do something. One way I motivate myself is getting a commitment buddy. That's someone I try to speak to on a regular basis. We share our plans for the day or the week.

I might say, "Today, I'm going to commit to going through old papers in my desk."

She might say, "Today, I'm going to commit to going to a Pilates class."

It's good to have someone to talk to about your plans, because then you're held accountable. It's sort of like making a plan to meet for lunch. You say what you want to do, and then you actually do it. And that boosts your self-esteem. Even if you don't finish the whole task or do less than you wanted, at least you did something.

Self-Reflection

Think of one or two people who could be your commitment buddy.

"The need for change bulldozed a road down the center of my mind." — Maya Angelou

Procrastination

When we feel down on ourselves because we put off doing the things we have to do, that's procrastination. It's understandable when it comes to doing the laundry. Yet when we continue to procrastinate again and again, we decrease our self-esteem because we're at a standstill.

My procrastination stems from perfectionism. I'm sometimes so afraid that I might do something imperfectly that I put off doing it at all.

However, when that pile of laundry gets bigger and bigger, we feel awful. That place of inaction isn't healthy for me because I feel like I'm not moving ahead with my life. Sometimes, when I'm in that place, I start thinking critical thoughts about myself. I condemn all my imperfections, fall into a swamp of self-pity, and wind up doing nothing. The longer I do nothing, the more self-pity I feel.

You can't feel self-esteem when you feel sorry for yourself. So there are several things you can do to stand up to your procrastination and nudge it out of the way so you can take action.

One way I beat procrastination is by promising to reward myself after I complete a task. If I do a load of laundry and then start my tax returns, let's say, I'll take a bubble bath later. Or I'll look at travel sites and dream about an exotic destination.

Another method is to set my timer for fifteen minutes and do this dreaded thing for only that long. Or, I'll listen to six songs while I do the dreaded thing and then stop when the music ends. That way, I don't get overwhelmed. I can't complete the task all at once, and I might hesitate before doing it again, but at least I'm making progress.

Finally, if I set up a routine, then I can do a job without giving it too much thought. When I clean the kitchen, for example, I always start from the left corner and work my way around. This way, I avoid the "Oh no! Where do I begin?" question that often used to plague me when faced with a pile of dishes and a mess in the kitchen. I use the same technique in other rooms too.

Stop the PLOMs

The opposite of self-esteem is self-pity. Poor Little Old Me. I used to have a list of all the people who'd wronged me. Jobs where I wasn't appreciated, folks who'd overlooked my birthday, and the boss who didn't give me a promotion.

Self-pity is a parasite that drains us of all positive get-up-and-go. We lose energy to move forward, and instead, we're pulled backward into the past or stay stagnant and don't move ahead. When I find myself slipping into self-pity, I try to be grateful for all I have instead of thinking about what I wish I had.

We need to stop asking, "Why me?" Or, "Why does this always happen to me?" When we ask, "Why me?" we stay in the position of victims. But if we ask, "What am I going to do about it?" we move to a position of power. We then plug ourselves into an electric current of positive energy.

I go from blaming others, the world, the weather, my family, my friends, or my boss, to asking, "What can I do to take action and boost my self-esteem?" I go from living in the problem to living in the solution. I can focus on how I can take care of myself to boost my self-esteem.

Self-Reflection

What makes you slip into self-pity? Can you appreciate all you have instead?

Where Energy Goes, Energy Flows

I was applying for a new job. I really wanted to get hired and had worked hard to prepare for a presentation I had to give. During the presentation, a dozen people listened to me intently, and everyone laughed at my jokes. Everyone except for one woman, who sat like a stone with a sour expression on her face. I kept looking at her, trying to get her to crack a smile. Her negative energy almost made me forget what I was supposed to say.

Where the energy goes, the energy flows. I had to pull myself away from even glancing in her direction and focus instead on the people who gave me positive feedback. I did get the job—no thanks to her—and, ironically, she quit a few weeks after I was hired.

I'll always remember her and be grateful. She taught me an important lesson: keep my mind away from people who make me doubt myself. To build my self-esteem, I want to be with people—both physically and mentally—who celebrate me and don't just tolerate me. I go where I feel the love. I go where I feel the warmth.

That's why I don't watch violent movies. I don't want to see the fights, the viciousness, the blood, or the gore. Building self-esteem means surrounding myself with things that boost my well-being. Self-protection is self-love. It means I have the right to reinforce my self-esteem with steel armor.

Self-Reflection

Is there someone in your life pulling you down? What can you do about it? Who makes you feel good about yourself?

The F-Word

No, not that *four*-letter word. This *three*-letter word: F-U-N.

Our self-doubt puts the brakes on any kind of fun we might have.

We think we don't deserve it. We think we have to earn it. We think we should be working or cleaning the house or taking care of other people. We've convinced ourselves that a life of purpose means always being serious. The doubter inside us will often say, "Nope, there's nothing I can do for fun today." Or, "Be realistic. Be serious. Life isn't all fun and games."

Yet fun is a multipurpose vitamin for our entire being. It's as important as using all the other tools to increase self-love. Having fun is a way to fill your own well, to boost your self-esteem. You don't always have to make to-do lists and check things off. Fun is a way to connect to yourself, nourish your essence, and show that little girl inside that you're worthy of having fun. You deserve it!

We spend so much of our time on self-help and self-improvement and self-awareness. All these are crucial pieces that fit the puzzle, but we also need to kick off our shoes, put away our journals, and dance in a field of clover.

Some of us think we can have fun only after we fulfill certain requirements. We think we have to earn pleasure and enjoyment. We're convinced that working nonstop is what mature, responsible people do.

However, we need enjoyment just like we need flavor in our food. We don't eat only for nutrition. We also eat for taste. Fun is as important as salt, pepper, cinnamon, and a wee bit of sugar. When we allow ourselves to have fun, we're telling self-doubt to take a hike.

Fun doesn't mean spending thousands of dollars we don't have on a pair of stiletto heels we'll wear once. It doesn't mean lying around on the sofa binging for hours. Fun isn't being self-indulgent and doing things that are bad. It could be as wild as parachuting out of an airplane or as simple as buying a package of colored pencils and a coloring book or a pad of blank paper. It could be having a picnic or putting on galoshes and walking through puddles. We can get creative or silly or adventurous. Fun is, just, well, it's freaking fun!

Self-Reflection

Can you make a list of ten things you can do to have fun? What can you do to have fun today? How can you plan to have fun another day?

CHAPTER FOUR

Letting Go of Expectations

*"To expect too much is to have a sentimental view
of life, and this is a softness that ends in bitterness."*
— Flannery O'Connor

What does an expectation have to do with loving ourselves? Plenty.

Expectations are the start of trouble. Part of learning to love ourselves is learning not to expect other people to behave how we think they should behave.

We get frustrated when we expect people to follow *our* script. We're not the director of a movie that everyone else is playing in. The people in our lives aren't actors in our movies. They're actors in their *own* movies, in which they have the starring roles.

If we expect others to act according to our script, those expectations might turn into unrealistic demands. It's like the woman who tells other people what she thinks devoted family members and loving friends should do. It is her unmet expectations, not other people, that lead to disappointments.

We can let go of the script. We can let go of the rules about how other people should behave. It isn't realistic to expect others to follow our script. They won't ever say exactly what we think they should say. When we have a script in my mind about how other people should act, we set them up for failure.

If we throw out the script, we'll see others realistically. We'll stop making demands and start accepting. We'll be more content with others and ourselves. That's the start of loving ourselves. At the same time, we can remember times when people expected things from us that we didn't always give them. Perhaps a friend wanted to meet with us more often, a relative was offended we had other plans for Thanksgiving, or a colleague felt snubbed because we talked more to someone else.

We can't read other people's minds, and they have no way of knowing what we feel inside. I'm thinking of Madeline, a single mother who sacrificed a lot to raise her son on her own—and she didn't let him or anyone else forget it. When he became a young adult, he went to college in another city, where he still lives. When Madeline's birthday rolled around one year, he didn't make plans to be with her, and she was very hurt.

"Did you ask him to be with you?" I asked.

"No!" she replied in a huff. "He should have known what I expected."

Yet nobody knows what we feel or want. It's our responsibility to tell them in a straightforward manner, without any hints or manipulation. We can't say, "I'm all alone on my birthday and I have nothing to do," then expect someone to jump in and rescue us.

If Madeline had spoken in a manipulative way to her son, he might have come to her—but only because he felt pity, guilt, and obligation.

"I've done so much for him," Madeline said. "It's the least he can do."

Mothers *do* sacrifice a lot for their children. We spend so many minutes, hours, and days of our lives taking care of them. We're just like penguins who stand in the freezing wind and snow, huddled around their babies. Parent penguins don't ask for anything in return from their offspring, nor should we. If we give love with strings attached, with secret expectations that our children will somehow pay us back or do for us in equal measure, we're setting ourselves up for disappointment. We can't have expectations and then secretly demand that our loved ones live up to them. They often don't even know what those demands are!

What we do need to do, however, is acknowledge our own needs. Once we know what we feel and want, we can consider our options. Madeline could have told her son directly, "I'd love to be with you on my birthday. Do you think you can come?" If he said no, she could have decided to visit him or made other plans.

So it's important that we stop expecting and start accepting.

It's our job to take care of our own needs. It's not other people's job to act according to what *we* think they should do, say, or give, yet we often react with self-righteousness and anger fueled by our secret expectations.

Loving ourselves means acknowledging our needs, communicating them, then letting go of our expectations. If we stop expecting and start accepting, we'll experience contentment and feel at peace with others and ourselves. If we let go of our expectations, we experience freedom.

Self-Reflection

Are there people in your life you expect things from? Do you make unreasonable demands on people? How can you now handle expectations in a self-loving way?

Resentments

Every expectation we have is a setup for possible disappointment. In a way, expectations are resentments just waiting to happen. An unmet expectation leads us to feel sorry for ourselves or get angry. That often loops into self-pity, which leads to resentment. It's a vicious cycle: expectation ... disappointment ... self-pity ... resentment.

Resentments are a dead end. They're an endless loop in our heads. Resentment comes from the French word *resentir*, which means to feel something again and again. Resenting what someone else did or didn't do and feeling anger fills our insides with corrosive thoughts. And this corrosiveness is dangerous. Indeed, resentments cause emotional pain and stress. In fact, more than 90 percent of all doctor visits in America are for stress-related complaints. According to the American Psychological Association, constant stress over a prolonged period of time contributes to long-term problems with the heart and blood vessels, as well as elevated stress hormones.

Resentments block out forgiveness, love, and hope, keeping us chained to events that happened long ago. These resentments drain us of love and fill our hearts with bitterness. Nobody wants to be around a bitter person, so we become lonely and full of self-pity, and that leads to more resentments.

Resentments … bitterness … pushing away other people … resentments … bitterness.

It's another vicious cycle.

If we don't give up our resentments, we continue drinking poison, hoping the other person will get sick.

Lily, a fashionable fifty-year-old woman, works in the mortgage department of a bank. Her customers appreciate her hard work and fun personality because at work she's able to hide the huge resentment she's been carrying against her ex-husband, who left her ten years ago. She still expects him to apologize for leaving her and marrying someone else. She continues to voice her bitterness to her children, friends, and family, chewing on this resentment like a rottweiler chewing on a bone.

After I heard her complaints, I suggested, "Pray for his happiness, health and prosperity."

"No freaking way!" she said. "I'm not going to pray for him. He ruined my life. He did something so wrong to me, and until he apologizes, I'll never forgive him."

"Can you at least pray for him through gritted teeth?" I asked.

"No, no, and no."

Lily's rancor festered inside her. This corrosive anger was filling her mind, heart, and soul, preventing her from feeling any joy. She was making herself sick with it. Literally. She had bad stomach pains.

"Can you pray only for the willingness to possibly pray for him?" I asked.

"Why?"

"Because you're tired of hurting," I said. "Because you need to move on with your life."

So each morning, she prayed for the willingness to open her mind just a crack so she could become willing to even consider praying for him. Slowly, very slowly, she began to push aside her own feelings and consider praying for him as the father of her daughters. That led her to feel a sliver of gratitude. After a while, she began praying for his happiness, health, and prosperity, and praying to be free of her own bitterness. She'd been waiting for her ex-husband to apologize, but instead she took the first step.

"My stomachaches went away," she reported to me. "How did that happen?"

"Because we can't wait for the person who wronged us to make amends," I explained. "Forgiveness isn't always between the person and us. It's between us and the Universe. We have to bypass the person and go directly to the source of all love and forgiveness."

It seems strange—and difficult. At first, we feel like we're being shortchanged because we didn't get the apology we wanted. Yet we can forgive without involving the other person, as difficult as it seems. And once we forgive, we're free. We can let go and walk away. Forgiveness isn't for the other person. It's for us. We don't need to wait for the other person to right the wrong. We right the wrong.

We love ourselves enough to channel love from the Universe. This sort of forgiveness can change our lives.

Self-Reflection

Is there someone you're holding a resentment against? Can you pray for the willingness to open your heart just enough to pray for further forgiveness?

Along with resentment comes mental criticism. I used to get upset when I felt my husband was criticizing me, until I realized I was doing the same thing back to him—but in my head. I wasn't saying things out loud, but my mind kept up a list of complaints about him. This didn't change him; all it did was fill my mind with judgments. So, each time I caught myself grumbling about him in my head, I'd quickly think of at least three things I appreciated about him. I was able to direct my mind into gratitude, and that immediately changed how I felt.

Loving ourselves means freeing our minds from that chatter of discontent. Then we can plug into the love. It means we're inching away from expecting things from others and to accepting other people exactly as they are. Accepting that what they can give us is exactly what they can give us. And that's okay.

Self-Reflection

When you have mental criticism, can you stop yourself and direct your thoughts to things you have that you can appreciate?

The Give-First Technique

If we really want to feel good about ourselves, we have to stop demanding that our desires be met according to how we want. Instead, we can start to do the very things we expect others to do for us.

This was the case with Kyla, a bubbly woman in her late twenties who teaches fourth grade in a public school. She gives her heart and soul to her rambunctious students. Each afternoon, she comes home feeling drained and wants her husband to do more for her.

"I want him to be understanding in the evening," Kyla said. "I want him to sometimes spoil me. I want him to hug me more. I want him to compliment me."

"Why don't you start then?" I asked.

"Start what?"

"Give first exactly what you want. Start being more understanding in the evening. Spoil him. Hug him. Compliment him."

Kyla wanted him to do these things first. But does it really matter in the long run?

No.

She started showing him exactly what she wanted, and he started reciprocating. Instead of getting angry when he left the toilet seat up, she started leaving the toilet seat up for him.

"He got a laugh out of that," she said.

Doing for her husband communicated to him what she wanted. And it helped her become more self-aware. She began thinking about what she wanted for herself and what she could do for others. Kyla said the give-first technique also helped her with her students. Instead of waiting for them to be courteous with her, she made it a point to be extra courteous with them, even—especially—with the more difficult ones. And it worked.

If we put aside the rather silly issue of who starts the give-first technique, it can spark miraculous changes in relationships.

Self-Reflection
What do you want from someone else? How can you use the give-first technique?

Remember algebra?

Let's talk about this equation: A + B = C. What happens when you change A? B might not change, but the end result, C, will change. That means, if we change, then we're going to get something different!

How often do we think the other person needs to change? We think it's the other person's fault if they don't meet our needs.

To love ourselves more, we need to examine our own attitudes. We might be walking around dissatisfied with life solely because other people aren't doing what we want. They aren't exactly what we'd like.

Critical thoughts about other people do serious damage to relationships.

Getting annoyed that other people don't do things as we want them to means we're constantly judging others and expecting them to live up to our standards. That's unrealistic, and almost childish, on our part. We must accept other people as they are and change ourselves.

The same is true when we ask for what we need in a straightforward, clear manner and people say no. Ouch! Just because they sometimes disappoint us doesn't mean they don't love us. It just means they want to do something else. We, too, don't always say yes to the people we love. When we say no, it sometimes means we're taking care of ourselves. We need to allow others the right to take care of themselves. Just as we can't do what other people expect of us all the time, we have to learn to accept when other people don't meet our expectations.

Self-Reflection

Have you asked someone to do something, and they said no? How did you feel? How did you feel when someone asked you to do something, and you said no?

Who Ya Calling Scrawny?

The final piece to releasing expectations is to have a sense of humor about it all. I heard a story about a woman who used to take her little son food shopping with her. While he sat in the grocery wagon, she picked out the nicest carrots for him. She liked thin, small carrots because she thought they tasted better.

Her son grew up. One day, he got angry at her and accused her of buying him "scrawny carrots."

"Scrawny carrots?" she asked. She'd spent time choosing what she thought were the best carrots, and her son saw them as scrawny. She thought she'd been doing something very nice for him, and it wasn't at all what he wanted.

We really don't know what other people want, and they really don't know what we want. Any time someone doesn't get me what I want, I think of the woman buying carrots she thought were slender and delicious but her son thought were scrawny and stunted. I can remember that people do the best they can to please us, and we do the best we can to please others. Expectations are a two-way street.

The most challenging part about doing this work on expectations is that it requires us to be completely honest. We must put down the magnifying glass we've been using to examine other people's faults and pick up the mirror. Loving ourselves is an act of naked honesty. We become self-aware. We recognize that it isn't only the other person who hasn't lived up to our expectations; we also play a role. What's our responsibility?

Loving ourselves means moving away from demands and expectations, and practicing self-awareness.

Self-Reflection

This is a three-part exercise to help you let go of expectations. Can you think of someone you expected something from that you didn't get? What was your past part in it? What can you do about it in the future?

Here's an example from a woman named Shannon:

When I moved to my sister-in-law's neighborhood, I expected her to invite my family to dinner more often than she has.

My part in the past:
- I never told her that I'd like to have dinner there more often.
- I assumed she knew that.
- I don't invite her to my house often.
- My husband and I sometimes argue, and I know it makes her uncomfortable.
- My kids sometimes get wild.

What I can do about it in the future:
- I can plan a dinner and invite my sister-in-law and family.
- I can try to not argue with my husband in public.
- I can try to accept that not everyone wants to be with me and find other people to have dinner with.

Once Shannon saw the issues on paper, she realized she could take some steps to change the situation.

"We cannot tell what may happen to us in the strange medley of life. But we can decide what happens in us—how we can take it, what we do with it—and that is what really counts in the end."
— Joseph Fort Newton

CHAPTER FIVE

Outgrowing Fear

"You get to the point where your demons, which are terrifying, get smaller and smaller and you get bigger and bigger." — August Wilson

---

There are a lot of acronyms for fear:

Forgetting **E**verything's **All R**ight
Future **E**vents **Al**ready **R**uined
Fully **E**mbracing **All R**eality
Fear **E**xcludes **All R**eason
and
F—k **E**verything **a**nd **R**un (gotta love this one)

My go-to slogan is **F**ace **E**verything **a**nd **R**ecover. I lived in fear around my mother. I was as hypervigilant as a German shepherd, sensing danger just by the way she put out her cigarette. If she ground it with her thumb, it was bad. If she left it burning in the ashtray, she wasn't too angry.

She passed away a while ago, and my fear of her is gone. But I'm still left with lingering fears. Fear about what I have to do. Fear that I'll be bad at it. Fear that I'll fail. Fear that I'll be humiliated. There are times when my knees are shaking and my thoughts are spiraling out of control with fear.

How do you turn that four-letter word *fear* into that five-letter word *faith*?

You hold your inner child's hand.

Every time I go to the gynecologist, I get petrified. I immediately become that helpless little girl lying on the examination table, feeling so vulnerable and about to get violated.

So before each exam, I use this visualization tool: I close my eyes. I picture myself standing in front of the situation I'm about to face. I picture my feet planted firmly on the ground. I picture myself with the little girl inside me—the little girl who was scared of the doctor, scared of her parents' fighting, and scared that a disaster could happen at any moment.

I tell that little girl, "I'm here with you now. I'll protect you. I won't let anyone hurt you. I've got your back. You're safe with me."

I visualize taking the little girl's hand in one of my hands. With my other hand, I reach for my Higher Power. It's connected to all the goodness, love, and strength in the Universe. My Higher Power is far stronger than that lower power, which is fear. And fear has nothing on my Higher Power.

I can do this.

There's an old saying that goes: "Courage is fear that has said its prayers." You might never be able to hit the delete button on fear, but if you say your prayers for courage, you can push it to the side. You can be afraid but still act. And sometimes when we act despite our fear, we grow even more.

Self-Reflection
Is there an upcoming situation you fear? Can you take your inner child's hand? What are some positive statements you can use?

We can—and must—do the hard things

I met a woman who told me she was raising baby chicks. She'd always wanted to do it, and one day she decided to try.

As she watched the baby chicks struggling with their hatching, she decided to peel back some of the eggshell to get the chicks out. The chicks she left alone kept pecking and pecking, and then they hatched.

And the chicks she tried to help? They never developed the muscles they would have used to crack open the shells themselves. They died. Her help damaged them. Her help actually killed them.

Imagine the chicks inside the shells. They were probably filled with fear. They were tweeting, "How am I going to ever get out of here? How will I be strong enough to crack open the shell? I can't ever accomplish this. I've never done anything like this before!"

Those chicks had to put aside all their little-chick fear, then they did the work. They found courage to break out of their shells only after they acted.

Act like a chick. You don't get any instruction manual that covers how to act bravely in life. You just have to act and find your bravery.

Outgrowing fear can happen only after we do the work. We pray for courage and go about doing the task. And only then can we burst out of our shell.

Today If I'm afraid of doing something, I remember that the only way to outgrow my fear is to begin the work.

There's no problem in front of us that's as great as the power behind us.

The Hero of My Own Story

When I think of a hero, I imagine Amelia Earhart in her airplane or Rosa Parks standing up against injustice just by sitting down. But we're all heroes of our own life stories! We might not battle an evil creature or have to slay a dragon, but we're heroes in our own right.

I've often brushed aside and minimized difficult situations I've had to endure, but it helps me to remember that I've been through a lot in life, and I've survived.

I've been lonely, scared, and lost. I've said good-bye to people I love. I've lost good friends and family. I've had my heart broken. I've felt abandoned.

There were times when I thought I wouldn't make it. When I didn't feel I had the armor, the special weapons, or the courage.

But I kept at it. I kept at my life, and I'm still here. I made it. I didn't give in or give up. I felt afraid a lot of times, but I moved forward despite the fear. And I survived. And I will again.

Each time I want to crawl back under the covers because I feel afraid, I remember that I can feel fear but still do something difficult. Thinking of myself as a hero is a loving way to help myself outgrow my fear.

Make a God Can

Some people call it a God Box. I call it a God Can, because God can.

I use a little tin box. Friends use ceramic jugs, a piggy bank, or a plastic container.

I write what I'm fearful of on a slip of paper and then put it in the God Can. Then I try to forget about it. Each time I catch myself obsessing over some fear or worry, I remind myself, "Oh yeah, that's in the God Can. God can."

It might take longer than I want. It might still be an ongoing situation. But I find myself less fearful if I write it down and give it to a greater power to sort out.

Once a year, I take out all the slips of paper. I'm often delightfully surprised because many of the things I was fearful about didn't come to pass. Other situations get resolved without any effort on my part.

I then have proof. Evidence. I can see all the times God has worked out challenges in my life and the lives of my loved ones.

Self-Reflection

Can you make a God Can and use it?

Develop Your Own Mudra

Mudras are symbolic gestures practiced with the hands and fingers.

If you connect your fingers in certain shapes, you can restore the flow of energy. There are traditional mudras in certain yoga practices. I encourage you to make your own.

When I'm fearful and want to calm myself down, I place the thumb of my left hand into the palm of my right hand, then clasp it gently. This gesture reminds me of when my children were little. They'd hold on to my thumb with their entire hand and feel comforted. I could feel their body relax.

When I'm in the midst of a difficult conversation and find myself getting upset, I put my hands in my personal mudra position and feel more at peace.

One of my friends has her own mudra. She puts her palms together, as she does in prayer, and keeps her hands on her lap. She says she can do this under her desk or at a table. Another friend rests her hands on her belly, the way she used to when she was pregnant and would connect to the baby inside her. And a third friend places one hand over the other the way her husband cups her hand before they fall asleep.

Experiment with a mudra that will steady you in times of fear. This is like a shield, a comfort, a safe zone. Once you find your own mudra, it's like you're home. If you breathe in deeply, feeling present, this position will be stored inside you as a place of safety. It's your comfort zone, no matter what's happening all around you.

Self-Reflection
Can you think of a mudra that will be helpful?

Today Just Might Be a Get-Through Day
Some days are full of goodness and peace. Other days are full of fear—what I call a Get Through Day. That's when we just have to get through the day as best we can. Maybe we're afraid of an upcoming talk with our boss; maybe we just moved and all our stuff is in boxes and we think we might have made the wrong decision; maybe we're afraid we have to make a move and don't know what to do.

Those are Get Through Days—days when we have to call on all our inner courage and do whatever we can to make the situation a little more tolerable.

We can try as hard as we can on those days to remember that we don't just go through challenges—we *grow* through them. We can try to use the experience as spiritual lessons. There will be days like this. Days when nothing makes sense. There are some painful times ahead. But we will get through them because we're in this thing called life together. We can support each other. We can remember that sorrow is halved each time we share it with someone.

On those days when we feel fear, we can remember to trust that life is unfolding exactly as it should. We think things should go faster, be different and better, then we come to understand that this day is exactly as it's supposed to be. There's a divine order to the Universe. What's happening now is exactly what's supposed to happen. We can dive into the moment when we're in the car, when we're in the office, or when the apartment is filled with boxes. We can breathe in deep and stay present. We can tell ourselves, "Oh yes, God is right here with me."

Self-Reflection

What can you do differently during a Get Through Day? What can you learn? How can you grow so that you get stronger?

Becoming Our Own BFF

While it's vital to have a best friend—or a few—it's also vital to be our own best friend.

Practicing self-care during fearful times eases our difficulties. When I feel afraid, I repeat to myself what my best friends tell me. I remind myself, "I'm braver than I feel! Fear and dread are lower powers, and they won't overwhelm me. Awful times have visited me before, and they'll most likely visit me again. But I can weather any storm that comes my way."

And just as farmers store grains for times of drought, we can store memories of all the times when God has come through for us. In times of fear, we can return to those memories and think about them, remembering that we've been taken care of before and will be taken care of again.

Some of us have suffered great losses. We might be able to focus only on a terrible memory rather than a positive one. Yet there's always something—the smallest thing—that might come from a tragedy. That's what we must train our minds to think of. We must be like a bird after a flood, searching for a dry branch or twig to alight on.

When we're full of fears, we can go to our storehouse of memories and find something to give us strength and hope.

Self-Reflection
Are you willing to try to speak to yourself like your best friend? Can you think of three times you were taken care of in the past? Can you put them in your memory vault and refer to them during times of fear?

Having Faith in the God of Our Understanding
There's a beautiful story about a woman who gets caught in a snowstorm. She's cold, tired, hungry, afraid. She's lost and doesn't know which way to go. She sees lights in the far distance, and she cries out to God, "God, where were you?"

And God answers, "Honey, turn around. You'll see only one set of footprints. I've been carrying you all along."

Wherever you are, whatever you have to do, and whenever you're afraid, remember there's only one set of footprints because God is carrying you. God has been carrying you all along.

Self-Reflection
How can you deepen your faith in your Inner Force or Higher Power to help you in times of fear?

CHAPTER SIX

Stopping Self-Doubt

"He that respects himself is safe from others;
he wears a coat of mail that none can pierce."
— Henry Wadsworth Longfellow

The more we love ourselves, the less we doubt ourselves. Our self-love is inversely proportional to our self-doubt.

I once drove in a car with Mike, a neighbor. I like him, even though he's a macho sort of guy and a Mr. Know-it-All. As we rode around a corner, his car tires screeched.

"Do you know you need air in your tires?" I asked.

"Nah," he said. "The car's just warming up."

"No. When you don't have air, your tires make noise. It's like they're crying out in pain."

"Oh yeah?" he said. "I bet you $10 I don't need air."

I hesitated. Self-doubt started to creep in. What did I know, anyway, about cars? Maybe I was wrong. I couldn't possibly be dumb enough to think I was smart enough to go up against Mike when it came to his car.

Why should I wager $10 on this?

Mike started whistling, already certain that he was right.

Only his boasting self-confidence pushed me into saying, "You got yourself a bet."

We drove to the nearest gas station. I waited while he checked the tire pressure. And I was right! His tires needed air. And he put in enough to make the screeching go away.

It's a challenge to replace self-doubt with trust in ourselves and our capabilities. Loving yourself means being able to believe in yourself. You might not win every bet or every race. And there are plenty of times when you'll be wrong. But you can use the following tools to help you grow away from that gnawing sense of doubt.

1. What People Say About You is None of Your Business

As we grow in self-respect, we trust ourselves more. This is illustrated by the following story.

A man and his son set off on a long journey to the market. They walked with their donkey behind them. Another man passed them riding on his horse and asked the father, "Why don't you let your son ride your donkey?"

The father placed his son on the donkey, and they continued on their way. They passed a family working in their fields. A young girl said, "Look at that lazy boy riding the donkey while his father is walking."

The man told his son to get off the donkey, and he climbed on. They passed a group of women, and one said, "What a selfish man! He rides the donkey while his son has to walk."

The man didn't know what to do now. He asked his son to climb up on the donkey with him. They passed a traveler on the road, who said, "That poor donkey is carrying both a father and son? That's way too much weight for that animal."

The man felt so sorry for the donkey that he and his son got off. They began to carry the donkey. But the donkey kicked them so violently that they released their hold, and the donkey ran away.

The father and son now had to walk the entire journey on their own.

When we listen to what other people say about us, we lose our connection to our inner voice. We take in their criticism and replace what could be our tenderness toward ourselves with their toughness.

People will always criticize us for one thing or another. That is their prerogative. Yet we don't have to let other people sway us. We need to ride on our donkey and continue our journey. We must not listen to the voices of those around us.

Self-Reflection
What is your takeaway from the story of the man and his donkey?

2. Other People's Truth Isn't Your Truth
We all have opinions based on our own experiences and perspective. We see things differently. There are people who shout the loudest and sound the most certain about their ideas, but their truth isn't necessarily our truth. We can trust ourselves and our own voice even more than we trust other people's.

When I was young, I relied on my mother's perspective. What she believed, I believed. Her opinion became the voice in my head. As I grew older, I came to rely on myself, developing my own ideas. It has taken a lot of work to separate her opinions from my own.

It was so easy to believe what other people—especially authority figures—told me. If someone said something cruel or critical about me, I immediately absorbed it and thought it was true. For far too long, I used other people's negative opinion as a weapon against myself.

Self-doubt for me is a code word for shame. It comes from that dark, sad place that was created when the doctor touched me and deleted me at the same time. So I still find myself doubting myself and my own truth.

But I'm learning. Like the man on the donkey, I can simply acknowledge that other people have opinions. If I decide to get off the donkey or stay on it, it's my choice. I can choose not to react out of shame and instead trust myself enough to make a decision that's right for me.

For those of us who have a secret—being sexually abused, for example—that shame never really leaves us. It hangs out in a corner of the soul, cobwebs and all, lurking and ready to reappear. There's no permanent solution to long-ago shame. We can't get rid of that shame forever, but we have the tools to push it away.

When you feel it, you can go to the mirror and say, "I love you, my sweet girl, and you did nothing wrong." You can hug yourself and say, "Oh yeah, this is that old, deep shame that's coming for a visit. Hello—and now get lost."

We can learn to trust our perceptions. If we're feeling self-doubt, we can explore the feeling and see if it's covering up shame from a childhood event. We can reach out to friends, as we've learned to, and we can ask for help from professionals and support groups.

When we become more aware of ourselves, we can recognize the pain inside us. We don't try to drown it in alcohol, food, painkillers, or sex. We learn to feel all our feelings. We learn that our feelings won't kill us. Pain is pain, but by loving ourselves and being with ourselves, we grow stronger than the pain.

When we love ourselves, we're inside our mind and heart and soul and body, so we know what's going on. If we have a stomachache, let's say, it might be triggered by doubt, fear, or stress. It could also be a sign that we feel the weight of shame that we're still carrying around.

You can never completely stop self-doubt, but when it comes, you can take steps to push it away again. Loving yourself is a daily practice. It's your job to do what you can each day to quench that fire of self-doubt with self-love. You can replace the shame with the reminder that you are pure and good.

Self-Reflection

What are some things you can say to yourself to stop the self-doubt and shame?

3. You Can't Give Away Your Glue

Everyone is born with their own glue. We use that glue throughout our lives to fix ourselves. We can't give away our glue to try to fix someone else. We need the glue to fix ourselves and take care of ourselves.

My mother often blamed me and said that if I'd been a better daughter, she'd feel happier. So I thought I was the cause of everyone's problems. And sometimes, when I was upset, I blamed my mother and father for my problems. I still have a hard time knowing what is or isn't my responsibility.

My mother tried to make me feel guilty for not living close to her. She used to tell me, "I need you. I don't have anyone else in my life. I can't live without you."

Those were the times I thought I needed to use my glue to fix her. I was filled with doubt, thinking I didn't deserve to live my own life when she was so miserable.

But we can't give away our glue, thinking we're responsible for fixing other people. I must take responsibility for my own life and let others take responsibility for theirs. I still get lost in self-doubt. So I need to remember that each of us is given glue to put together all the scattered pieces of ourselves.

Self-Reflection

Do you have a relationship in which you feel obligated to give away your glue? How do you feel saying no to that person?

4. Put On Your Own Oxygen Mask First

In an emergency on an airplane, flight attendants instruct passengers to put on their own oxygen masks before helping anyone else. At first, it seems counterintuitive. It seems that parents should help their children before they help themselves. But if we don't take care of ourselves first, we can't take care of anyone else.

The same is true for lifeguards. If a lifeguard saves someone and the two of them are about to smash into rocks, the lifeguard is instructed to let the other person take the injury. The lifeguard needs to make self-protection their priority in order to save both of them.

This mandate doesn't make sense for those of us who are accustomed to self-doubt. We can't imagine even thinking about saving ourselves before we save those around us.

Danielle is a landscape designer who likes to be outside, in the quiet, among the trees. It could be because she had a difficult childhood. Her mother became sick when Danielle was in elementary school. By the time Danielle was ten, she was already running the house. Her father began to rely on her to take care of the house as well as her three younger siblings. She learned from an early age that it was her job to put other people's needs ahead of her own. Whenever she thought about doing something nice for herself, self-doubt trickled in, and she'd think she shouldn't.

"I lost my connection to myself because I was so busy thinking about everyone else," Danielle said. "Every time I wanted to do something, I was filled with doubts about whether I deserved it. I also didn't feel right thinking about myself and feeling good when my mom was so sick."

One part of shedding self-doubt is acknowledging that it's okay to have needs. The other part is making sure you meet those needs. Danielle learned to put on her own oxygen mask before she put on someone else's. As you can see, if you put yourself at risk, you can't save anyone. So it's imperative that you first save yourself.

Self-Reflection
Can you take care of yourself first?

5. Don't Let Guilt Feed Your Doubt
We feel guilty when we do something wrong. But interestingly enough, sometimes we feel guilty when we do something right for ourselves.

If we're used to never saying no and always doing things for our loved ones, we feel guilty when we start saying no. Others might tell us how selfish and terrible we are, and we begin to doubt our own goodness. Guilt can cause us to lose our trust in ourselves and feed our self-doubt.

If we want to stop being used as a doormat, we have to get up off the floor. People might try to manipulate us and say that if we really loved them, we'd do this or that. They might try to guilt us into changing our mind. Yet if we work on trusting ourselves and listening to that little voice inside us, we can banish the guilt. If we banish the guilt, self-doubt will also vanish.

We can remind ourselves that when we forget about ourselves while trying to please people, we wind up with nothing.

6. Ask for Help

When we're full of self-doubt, we can ask for help. We can turn to other people for a reality check. Our friends see us in our best light. When we're confused, we can ask them for clarity and perspective. When we're feeling low, we can turn to them and ask them to hold our hand through that dark tunnel of doubt.

Some of us grew up feeling like we had to put other people's needs first. Others—like me—come from a family that abides by the acronym, **F**orget **A**bout **M**yself, **I** **L**ove **Y**ou. It was difficult to ask for help because I felt I should forget about myself and concentrate on helping my parents and sister.

It's taken me a long time to feel worthy enough to ask for help. Now I know I deserve it. I don't have to hint or wait for people to guess what I need. I can ask.

7. Have a Plan A and Also a Plan B

We realize that we need help and can't do it alone, so we reach out. However, the first person we ask says no, so we might dive into feeling rejected. Then we start feeling sorry for ourselves.

"You see what happened?" we might say. "I asked for help, and I was shot down! That only shows I shouldn't ask for help."

Our self-esteem plummets and our self-doubt gets jacked up like a car in an auto body shop. We interpret what just occurred to mean that we should go it alone. But it only means that we need a backup plan.

Rejections are part of life. We learn to accept them more easily when we have a contingency plan. Then, when people say no, we can turn to someone who will say yes: "Yes, I'll be happy to help you." "Yes, I'll be right over." "Yes, please call me so we can talk."

Having a plan A and a plan B is also good in other situations. For example, if we make plans to go to a concert with someone who always cancels at the last minute, we can ask someone if they mind being on standby.

Or, if we know that someone is always late, we can have a backup plan and arrange something to do while we're waiting.

Self-doubt doesn't have to paralyze you. You have choices. You don't have to continue being a victim. You'll be able to adjust your internal barometer when you make alternative plans.

Self-Reflection
Can you think of people you'd be willing to ask to be your plan B?

8. Fill Your Own Well

Before we feel love for ourselves, we sometimes search around for ways to remove our self-doubt. We feel unworthy, so we latch onto a man, a woman, a child, a job, a new sweater, or a piece of chocolate truffle cake. We think that if we have one of these people or things, we won't feel self-doubt. But if we depend on someone or something outside ourselves, self-doubt returns like snow in the winter or sunshine in the summer. Nothing can permanently fill us up. The relationship ends, the job is just a job, the chocolate cake is eaten, and the self-doubt lingers.

We must learn to fill our own well. Each time we act as if we respect ourselves, then we nudge away the self-doubt.

Self-Reflection
How can you fill your own well? How can you learn to take care of yourself even more?

CHAPTER SEVEN

Making Decisions

"Decision is a risk rooted in the courage of being free."
— Paul Tillich

I was in my twenties. I'd just bought a new bikini with ruffled fringes on the top and bottom, and I brought it home to model for my first husband. He told me it would have been a lot nicer if there wasn't a fringe.

I wanted his approval so much that I took the bikini out into the hallway of our apartment building. With a pair of scissors, I started cutting off the fringe. The bikini now looked like it had a crude seam on the top. It looked so bad that I got angry and cut the bathing suit into pieces and threw it down the building's incinerator.

That's how bad I was at making decisions. Without self-love, my decision-making process was based on what other people said. I rarely stopped to think about what I really wanted. Where was *I* in the decision-making process? What happened to me?

To create the life we want, we need to learn how to make decisions based on self-love. We can consider our loved ones' needs, but we must still honor our own. Of course, we must often compromise and meet other people halfway, but it's important to learn how to make decisions from a place of self-love and not based on getting other people's approval.

We learn to make decisions in a rational manner. Our decisions become well thought out and reflect our growing self-esteem and confidence. To make a positive contribution to our own life, we need to learn how to make appropriate decisions.

This fear of shopping still overwhelms me at times. The other day, for example, I went to buy an outfit for a family event. In the dressing room, I looked at myself in the mirror. I wasn't alone in there; it seemed my whole family was in there with me!

I could hear my husband saying I should buy something tighter, my mother saying the fabric looked cheap, my sister saying it wasn't stylish enough, and one of my sons saying the fashion industry is one of the biggest polluters and I should buy clothes only in thrift stores!

I sat down and closed my eyes. In my mind, I thanked each of them for their opinion, then I said the dressing room was for one person only. I had to really concentrate on what I wanted. I had to ask myself, "Which outfit makes me feel like a woman of grace, beauty, and dignity? What would make me feel like I'm wearing a dress befitting a royal daughter of a king?" And then I asked myself, "What dress do I really want?" I really felt close to myself—close to that little girl inside me. And then I chose a dress.

And I really don't care if these other people don't like it, because *I* like it.

Maybe some women go into a store, buy a dress, and don't think twice about what other people will say. Maybe they have enough self-love inside them. But for those of us who are just starting to feel self-love, making decisions (even a small one like buying an outfit) could be challenging.

I often wish I could look down the road and see what the outcome of my decision will be, but we get only enough light to see just a little portion of the road. We can't see further than right now. We can't know what the future holds. Yet we want to make a perfect decision—not only for right now but for months from now. We can make a decision based only on the knowledge we have at the moment. We can't predict what will happen next.

So how do we make a decision in a loving-ourselves sort of way? First, we need to remember that "Figure it out yourself" isn't loving. I've learned a variety of tools to use to make decisions.

Invite Someone to Talk Things Over

I try to invite someone I trust. Someone who will listen to me rather than tell me what I "should" do.

When I was deciding between two jobs, instead of panicking, I sat down with a friend, Susannah. She and I often help each other. I like to write things down. She prefers to speak from the heart. Together, we made a list:

- What I like about Job 1
- What I like about Job 2

- What I don't like about Job 1
- What I don't like about Job 2

Then Susannah and I tallied up the numbers. Each thing I liked got a positive point. Each thing I didn't like got a negative point. As I looked it over on paper, I talked about each item, thinking about the positive and negative aspects of each job. Susannah was able to help me start thinking about making my decision in a more rational manner, debating whether it was worth taking Job 1 because it paid more money. I put aside what my husband would say ("Go with Job 1 because it pays more money") and put aside what my son would say ("Don't take the job with the longer commute because it would increase your carbon footprint"). I stopped thinking about what anyone else would say. This is why I like Susannah. She just listens to me and doesn't offer her opinion.

"You're your own best expert," she always tells me.

God doesn't speak to us in code. The answer is one of the following:

- Yes
- No
- Wait
- You gotta be kidding!

So once I had the list, I just lived in the question—Job 1 or Job 2?—for a while. That meant I decided to simply be in uncertainty.

Not knowing might be uncomfortable, but it's important that we stay with our discomfort long enough to get closer to making a decision.

I looked around and listened. I thought maybe I'd hear a song that had words that spoke to me. Or maybe I'd meet someone with a similar job who nudged me this way or that.

I also decided to listen to the signs inside me. I paid attention to my body. How did I feel? Did I feel a slight headache when I thought of the commute to Job 2? Did my ulcer act up when I considered the amount of work in Job 1? Our body holds a lot of answers. If we're still and listen, we can understand ourselves better and figure out what we really want instead of what we think other people want us to want.

You're Gonna Make Mistakes

An airplane pilot doesn't fly straight from Alaska to Hawaii. A pilot goes a bit this way and then a bit that way to respond to weather conditions.

Likewise, we sometimes make mistakes with our decisions, veering a little in one direction and then a little in the other to accommodate life.

I decided not to make a decision right away, in crisis mode. It's better to wait and decide from a place of self-love, not worrying what others think. So I took the following actions:

- Talk it over.
- Pray on it.
- Write on it.

- Sleep on it.
- Wait on it.

I started to feel the answer come to me in the quiet, strong core of myself. But I still didn't trust myself. I was so scared I'd make the wrong decision. I was also scared people would criticize the decision I made. I wrote a letter to God, who wrote back: "Oh honey, even if you make the wrong decision, I'll take care of it for you."

And that made it easier for me to make a decision. I knew I could use whatever happened as a spiritual lesson.

When I felt in my belly that it was the right move, I was able to act. I felt a sense of relief and boldness. I felt free. Free from everyone else's opinions. Free to follow my intuition.

And that's true freedom.

Remember That You Did the Best You Could at the Time

Even if you use all these tools and follow all these steps, you may still make the wrong decision. You may look behind you now and see things in the past that you just couldn't see at the time.

Hindsight is always 20/20. We're human. Making mistakes is part of life. It just is.

We can be gentle with ourselves. We can remember that we made the best decision we could at the time with the information we had. There's simply no guarantee that life will go according to our plans. As the saying goes, "Men make plans, and God laughs." We might have gathered all the information and still … Well, life gets lifey.

I knew I might outgrow one job and feel I should have taken the other. But I also knew I couldn't get to an even better job down the road until I did one of these other jobs first. We can't skip ahead without doing what we're required to do. That also means making decisions and making mistakes. Maybe we need to make a mistake in order to grow. Maybe it's only when we make a mistake that we can begin to get new answers.

In the end, after praying about it, writing about it, and talking about it, I chose the job that paid less and required me to work less. I made the right decision for myself.

Ruth Bader Ginsburg said, "So often in life, things that you regard as an impediment turn out to be great, good fortune." Our obstacles, our wrong decisions, might be the very things that lead to our ultimate good. We never know what's in store for us. All we can do is make the best decisions that we can today, and tomorrow will take care of itself.

Self-Reflection

Is there a decision you have to make? Do you want to write things down or talk it over with someone? What do you feel in your body? Can you write a two-way prayer?

CHAPTER EIGHT

Practicing Acceptance

"Now I realize that the trees blossom in Spring and bear fruit in Summer without seeking praise; and they drop their leaves in Autumn and become naked in Winter without fearing blame." — Khalil Gibran

Learning how to accept things exactly as they are—and not how we would like them to be—is one of the most difficult lessons to learn in life. Even as I try so hard to love myself, life is still challenging. I work diligently to improve my attitude. *Life should get easier*, I think. *Do I have to learn another lesson? Do I have to go through another struggle?* I want things to be, well, how I want things to be. Accepting life on life's terms, just as it is, is a daily challenge.

Searching for love for ourselves exactly as we are is a search for acceptance. Not just acceptance of ourselves, but of life itself. I begin to accept that I'm exactly who I'm supposed to be and that my life is exactly how it's supposed to be.

People appear in my life when I'm ready to learn new lessons. When they disappear, I'm ready to learn different lessons. Every time I think, *I thought I learned this already*, I'm ready for a deeper healing. Deeper acceptance. The lessons never end. Practicing acceptance is a course that runs our whole lives and from which we never graduate.

Here are some ways you can practice acceptance.

Make an ABC Gratitude List

"If the only prayer you said in your whole life was, 'thank you,' that would suffice." – Meister Eckart

I used to be one of those women who was never satisfied with just about anything or anyone. I was always thinking of what could have been better about a movie or a homecooked dish, or how I could have said something different. It was hard for me to focus on the good; I was always tweaking what was bad and trying to improve it. I wanted perfection from everything and everyone (including myself).

These days, I'm a lot less hard on people (including myself). Instead of looking at what's wrong, I try to focus on what's right. It helps me in times of trouble or stress to have a gratitude list. Learning to be grateful for the smallest things in my life makes all of my life more wonderful. I try to not take things for granted, such as being able to smell or hear or taste my food. Seeing how blessed I am helps me feel like my life is worthwhile.

Sometimes, when I'm feeling blue and everything seems bad, I force myself to make an alphabetical gratitude list. This helps me veer my thoughts away from my troubles. I start with A:

- Alive! I'm alive.
- Breathe! I can breathe without an oxygen machine.
- Cozy! I've got a cozy blanket.

And I go all the way to Z.

Once, I had not one but two flat tires after I left a parent meeting at my kids' school. It was late at night, there were no cell phones back then, and I had to wait for someone to come help me. I was hungry and tired. I took a scrap piece of paper and started writing an ABC gratitude list. It kept my mind off the problem, and it seemed that just as I'd completed the list, help suddenly appeared.

Another time, I spilled orange juice all over the floor, and a sticky, sugary, pulpy mess seeped everywhere. On my hands and knees, I started to feel sorry for myself, thinking, *My kids don't appreciate all I do for them! My husband will say I'm too clumsy!* Then, as I was cleaning up near the refrigerator, it suddenly hit me: I had a refrigerator! I had oranges. I had so much to be grateful for!

When I have to wash a lot of dirty dishes in the sink, I try to feel grateful that I have dishes. Grateful that I have the food that made the dishes dirty. Grateful that I don't need to haul water to wash the dishes.

Gratitude is like math: it multiplies our blessings. It pushes away self-pity and opens the door to acceptance. When I stop discounting all I have, I can truly acknowledge my bounty.

Self-Reflection
What can you write on your alphabetical gratitude list?

"Life holds so much—so much to be so happy about always. Most people ask for happiness on condition. Happiness can be felt only if you don't set conditions." — Arthur Rubinstein

Accept the Idea That Life Isn't Fair

I used to think that because I've followed all the rules, tried so hard, and been nice to others, life should reward me with a lot of goodies. But life doesn't follow *my* rules. Things that happen are often hard for us to understand. That's when we must repeat these words of acceptance:

Life is exactly how it is, not how we think it should be.

When someone once asked tennis great Arthur Ashe why God selected him to have AIDS, which he contracted from a tainted blood transfusion following a heart operation, he replied that 50,000,000 children started playing tennis, 5,000,000 learned to play tennis, 500,000 learned professional tennis, 50,000 came to the circuit, 5,000 reached the Grand Slam, 50 reached Wimbledon, 4 reached the semifinals, 2 reached the finals, and when he was holding the cup in his hand, he never asked God, "Why me?"

"Why me?" is the question we pose only when we have a problem. I used to think it wasn't fair that my mother was alcoholic and difficult, but then another thought came to me. It also wasn't fair that I'm healthy and I don't suffer from any diseases. When it came to all those blessings, I never asked, "Why me?" I've learned that it's important to remember that life distributes its share of sorrows and joys to all of us, although it's true that some are luckier than others. We hear children sometimes say, "But that's not fair." And they're right.

My husband lost his mother when he was sixteen. He lost his father when he was twenty. He learned this lesson at an early age. Life just isn't fair. We won't understand everything; some things just don't make sense. But we need to practice acceptance.

Don't Compare and Despair

Remember that stuffed bunny rabbit I bought? After a while, I also bought a stuffed elephant. Each animal is beautiful and unique in its own way. The elephant has many gifts, and so does the bunny rabbit. There's no competition.

Yet I often forget this fact and compare myself to other women. I start thinking it's a pageant and there can be only one Miss America, only one with a crown. But that's scarcity thinking. It's forgetting there's abundance in the Universe and we each have our special beauty. There's no such thing as number 1.

Even if there are thousands of people on the beach, there's enough sunshine for all of us. We can each turn our face up to the light.

I sometimes look at another woman's photos on social media, for instance, and feel a pang of jealousy. It looks like she's having so much fun and her life is so good. I forget not to compare and despair, and suddenly, my acceptance level plummets. But envy is really a hostile form of self-pity. It means I'm feeling sorry for myself and having a pity party at someone else's expense.

I know that all of us have problems and nobody has a perfect life. Every woman has her own story of triumphs and troubles, her own difficulties. I try to not compare my insides with another woman's outsides because I really don't know the challenges she faces. So, instead of feeling envious, I try to keep my focus only on my life and all I have. If I find myself slipping into feeling sorry for myself, I make another gratitude list. Instead of looking at others and thinking about what I lack, I can focus again on all I have. This is practicing acceptance.

Remember That This Too Shall Pass

"This too shall pass" sounds like a cliché, but these four words help us accept that whatever is overwhelming us right now—whatever seems hopeless and wrong—won't last forever. At some point, the fires will stop raging, the floodwaters will recede, and the winds will stop blowing. We will get a break. The right people will show up to enhance our journey.

If we practice patience, we can stretch our acceptance. What we're going through is what we must go through today. The Universe has a plan, and we're all a part of it. We're just where we need to be.

Even if we're in a storm, we can look up at the glimmering drops of rain that fall from the heaviest clouds. We can see the stars glimmering in the darkest night. We can practice accepting the idea that perhaps the darkness was placed within us so that we find our inner strength and work hard to transform it into light.

Know That the Life You Have Is the Life You Have

There's a woman on a sailboat about to set out to cross the Atlantic Ocean. She's traveling the world, hoping to beat her personal record. She sees a yacht and thinks, *Wow, it would be so nice to be on that yacht. But then again, I really don't know who's inside the yacht. Are the people even nice? Would I have fun with them? No, I won't envy that yacht.* Then she sees an inflatable rubber boat and at first feels a wee bit superior. She's on a sailboat, and they're on this puny boat. Then she thinks, *I won't scorn that boat because I have no idea what wonders the owner of this boat has seen. I don't know its journey.* She comes to understand that the boat she has is the best boat for her. It's the boat she has.

She has gained acceptance.

> ### Self-Reflection
> What can you do to enhance your acceptance of
> what you have and who you are?

Feel All Your Feelings

Before I started on this journey toward being more loving to myself, I was scared to feel my feelings. I'd frozen many of my emotions in childhood because they were too painful. I almost felt that my feelings would kill me. They were that painful.

But feelings aren't facts, and they can't kill me. None of my feelings are wrong or bad. Some are more pleasant, some are less pleasant.

When I'm feeling all my feelings, it means I'm practicing acceptance. I still shy away from emotions that are difficult to handle—like anger or hurt—because I want to feel only the good stuff. Yet I can't pick and choose. I must accept all my emotions, feel them completely, and learn to let them go. That's the only way we can learn to love all of ourselves.

We might think each emotion has a different nozzle. We believe that if we shut off the nozzle that contains pain, for example, we can avoid it. We try to turn off the negative emotions so we feel only the positive ones.

Yet all our emotions come out of one nozzle, and when we freeze *some* of our feelings, we freeze everything. Eventually, our entire inner self gets frozen. That was what happened to me. I was emotionally numb. I couldn't feel pain, but I couldn't feel joy either.

Growing in love for ourselves enables us to start melting the frozen parts inside us. If we don't feel those buried feelings, they'll continue to haunt us. They'll control us, even if we think we're controlling them. We come to understand that we're only as sick as the secrets we keep, and sometimes those secrets are our powerful, underground emotions. Members of Overeaters Anonymous say, "It isn't what we're eating—it's what's eating us." We have to uncover those feelings and let them out.

Loving ourselves means being willing to express our feelings. We can feel happy and express it in numerous ways that feel good to us. We can feel a deep ache that has been buried and ask for help from a friend or a professional to guide us through a difficult time. We can identify our painful emotions, feel them, then accept those feelings, process them, and let them go.

Self-Reflection
Is there an emotion you've been avoiding? Is there something eating you?

No feeling should be pushed away because it seems like a bad feeling.

When I was little and told my mother that I hated one of the girls in the neighborhood, she scolded me, saying, "That's not nice." So I learned to stuff feelings that didn't seem nice. I wanted to be a good girl, and good girls didn't have feelings that weren't nice.

Yet I now know that all feelings are legitimate. They're simply our truth.

Feeling all our emotions and accepting them means we love ourselves. All of ourselves. I no longer hate people, because that word is too violent for me. I've learned that I don't have to spend time with people I don't necessarily like. I sometimes decide I don't want to be around the person, or I decide to spend time with them because they might be able to teach me a spiritual lesson. Maybe the lesson is accepting them. Maybe the lesson is remembering that we don't always get what we want from other people. In every case, we can learn something when we feel all our feelings and then decide what to do.

And that girl in my neighborhood? I don't know what happened to her. I hope she's had a good life.

Self-Reflection

What can you learn from someone you don't necessarily like? How can you grow?

Another Version of the Serenity Prayer

God, grant me the serenity to accept the people I cannot change; the courage to change the one I can and the wisdom to know it's me.

This version of the Serenity Prayer helps us remember to practice accepting other people just as they are. This is one of the most difficult parts of acceptance. Sometimes we think that if we only found that one word or that one phrase, we could change the screws in someone else's head. We think we can get through to them. We try to say it one way, and if they still don't change, we try to say it another way, using different words. But we can't change other people no matter what we say or do. That's why we ask for acceptance. It isn't an easy task. Some people drive us crazy. Others disappoint us.

Nicole is an energetic thirty-something aerobics instructor who went to visit her father a few days before her birthday. He'd invited her over so they could celebrate together. In her mind, she was thinking (hoping) that he'd make a special dinner, including a cake. As she was driving to his house, he called and asked if she wanted a salad.

A salad? she thought. *It's my birthday, and all he's going to make me is a salad?*

She knew then that she could also forget the cake.

Her first reaction was anger; she wanted to turn around and drive away. Then she thought she'd walk into his house and "give him a piece of my mind." Her third reaction was saying this Serenity Prayer. "God, grant me the serenity to accept the people I cannot change." She realized this was his pattern; he simply didn't know how to give her what she dreamed a father would give. That was just how he was. She could either get mad or accept him for who he was.

We don't always like the people we're supposed to love. So we don't go to them hoping things will be different. It's like going to a hardware store to buy an ice cream cone with sprinkles. Learning to love ourselves means we learn which people to go to for a celebration. With other people, we can practice acceptance, releasing them to be themselves.

Self-love extends outward, and we no longer stay trapped in expectations that lead to resentments. From that place of loving ourselves, we can accept others. That leads us to serenity, and in the serenity, we find more love.

"When you are offended at anyone's fault, turn to yourself and study your own failings. By attending to them, you will forget your anger and learn to live wisely." — Marcus Aurelius

Self-Reflection

How can you use this version of the Serenity Prayer?

Accepting Our Mistakes

Accepting ourselves means embracing ourselves, both the medals we've won and the mistakes we've made. As the funny saying goes, none of us gets out of life alive. And none of us goes through life without making a mistake or two along the way.

We all make mistakes—big mistakes and little ones. The key is accepting that mistakes are part of the human experience. We're all imperfect. Perfectly imperfect.

If we've made a mistake, we can apologize and try to change our behavior so we don't make the same mistake again. But it isn't healthy to keep staring at the past and wishing we could have done it differently. Whatever mistakes we made, we did the best we could at the time. We can't change the past.

In our new spiritual way of looking at life and loving ourselves, we now know that we can recycle the mistake and use it as a valuable lesson to help someone else who's hurting. Our experience enables us to say to someone, "Oh yeah, I made that mistake too."

It's important to say we're sorry. But what isn't healthy for those of us who still aren't completely sure of ourselves and our worth is to think we need to repeat the apology over and over again. We can't chase people who refuse to accept our apology. If someone won't forgive us after we've made our amends, we can let them go and forgive them for holding on to their resentment. We can stop feeling guilty about our errors.

You don't have to keep beating yourself up. You would have done better if you could have.

When you accept your own mistakes, it's easier to accept others' mistakes. You'll lose your smugness and stop gripping the halo around your head. You can look at your own mistakes and not focus on the mistakes of others. You'll stop saying, "Oh, I would never do that." Or "I would always do this." You'll remember that practicing acceptance is the only way you can find a sense of peace with yourself and the world.

Self-Reflection
If you made a mistake with someone, do you owe an apology?

CHAPTER NINE

Our Family History

---

*"We are given the parents who will serve as
our soul's teachers."* — Ariel B. Solomon

I was translating documents into English from French, a language I studied in college. I was getting paid by the hour. There was a part of the document that I hadn't been told to translate. But I decided to translate it without speaking to my boss. Not only was it interesting, but translating it also meant I would get paid more money. In the end, realized I was wrong, apologized to my boss, and told her to pay me only for what I'd been supposed to do.

She didn't hire me for another job after that because I'd lost her trust. I felt terrible. I talked things over with a friend, who asked me, "What motivated you to do that?"

"Fear," I blurted out. "Fear I won't have money." Then I paused. I always had enough money to pay my bills. I lived frugally but comfortably. I never worried about where my next meal was coming from. And yet I had an irrational fear about losing money.

Where did that come from? It seemed like a very deep, old fear that was almost bigger than I was.

To work through my difficulties with money issues, I attended a workshop on family constellations. The idea of family constellations is growing in popularity because more and more people are becoming aware of the influences of their family's history on their own lives, even if it has never been spoken about.

I delved into the history of my grandparents on my mother's side. They were immigrants to America. My grandfather worked very hard and became a police lieutenant. They had five children. When he died of a sudden heart attack when my mother was five, my grandmother was plunged into poverty. She struggled to support herself and her children the rest of her life.

My mother became a successful businesswoman, driven by her difficult childhood. Yet toward the end of her life, she also lost everything.

It dawned on me that I was reliving my grandmother's fear of not having enough money, which was passed onto my mother and then to me. My deep fears that what happened to them could happen to me continue to influence me.

The idea of family constellations means that our family's history and our ancestors' struggles are stored inside us. If it's hysterical, it's historical, as the saying goes.

You might be unconsciously motivated to do things because of struggles in your family's past. You're a link in your family's chain, which can hold you in bondage to the past. You might feel like you're carrying a heavy weight, dragged down by the past, and not even be aware of it.

Self-Reflection

Are there secrets in your family's past? A crime that someone in your family committed? Or crimes that were committed against people in your family? Were people in your family killed in a war? Was there betrayal? The death of a young child? An arduous journey? Was someone forced to put a baby up for adoption? Did your great-grandparents leave their birthplaces and never see their families again?

So much of what we do is automatic, and we're not even aware that we're doing it. To love ourselves, we also have to set ourselves free from the chains that bind us to the past.

Here is one more example.

Jordana's father was a pilot who was killed in an accident when she was little. Her mother never remarried, and Jordana took on the role of acting like her mother's emotional spouse. As many children do, Jordana wanted to take away her mother's pain. She married a man whose brother died when he was a little baby. Jordana's family history matched her husband's. Both were drawn to each other, both understood the other without even knowing why. They both were trying to comfort their parents and take the place of the lost family member. They both put aside their own childhoods to deal with grief.

There are a variety of exercises you can do to help free yourself from history so you can understand—and love—yourself more.

Some exercises include exploring how you might blow up and have out-of-proportion reactions, deal with illnesses in different parts of your body, find a sense of belonging, and discover hidden fears. You can also consult a professional in family constellations.

Meanwhile, you can also develop simple statements that affirm your healing. Mine is, "I know I'll always be taken care of."

Jordana, who was dealing with grief over her father, went to the cemetery where he was buried and read a letter she wrote to him. She said out loud, "You're living inside me. I'll make the most out of life."

There are many ways to become a link in a healing chain for our families—a chain that doesn't bind us with its sorrow but releases us with its love. We're freed when we know what happened in the past and then can face the future.

We love ourselves more fiercely when we know what might cause our self-hatred. We find strength and relief. Our bodies are created from the DNA of our parents and their parents before them. Our ancestors are linked to us not only physically but also spiritually. We honor them by remembering. We honor and love ourselves when we acknowledge them, thank them, and then move on.

In researching our family history, we don't blame anyone for our present pain. We received the parents who were right for us. Our parents were chosen for us so we could learn important lessons to grow and heal—both us and them.

This may seem unbelievable when we think of parents who were abusers, alcoholics, abandoners, or addicts. Yet the parents who gave us life must be considered the ones who are best for us.

They are our best teachers; they are the ones picked out to serve us the most powerful life lessons. When we accept that they were the ones chosen to be our teachers, we start to grow.

We honor them by remembering. We honor and love ourselves when we acknowledge them and thank them. We can say something like, "I accept the life you've given me, and I'll do my best to live it to the fullest."

Self-Reflection

Have you discovered a family secret that has influenced you? Can you think of something to do to connect to a family member? Is there a statement you can say that will help you in times of discomfort?

CHAPTER TEN

Healing Relationships

"We are quick enough at perceiving and weighing what we suffer from others, but we mind not what others suffer from us." — Thomas à Kempis

---

As I grow to love myself more, it has become easier to accept myself—the qualities I'm proud of and the less favorable qualities that I'm working to improve.

Healing my relationship with myself is the first step, and as I establish a healthy, loving relationship with my own self—learning to care for myself with tenderness and compassion—I can have better relationships with others.

Sick people attract sick people; healthy people attract healthy people. In the past, I chose friends who reminded me of my mother. They were often depressed, and I felt it was my job to cheer them up. I gave away my glue, thinking I could help them and fix them. As I became healthier and happier, I wanted to find friends who were also doing their best to find joy in life. I stopped wanting to be around miserable people. They no longer had any appeal for me. I didn't want to try to fix them. I didn't want their approval. I no longer confused their needing me with their loving me. These days, when I meet a woman like that, my inner alarm starts beeping: STAY AWAY!

It's a primary truth that our relationship with others reflects our relationship with ourselves. If we don't know how to listen to ourselves, we'll choose people who don't listen to us, and we, in turn, won't listen to others. If we don't know how to care for ourselves, we'll choose people who can't care for us either. If we grow in understanding that we're perfectly imperfect and make mistakes, then we can love people who are also perfectly imperfect. We become more accepting when they make mistakes, and we can keep on loving them. When we become less hard on ourselves and less judgmental, we're also less critical of others. We learn to treat ourselves well, then we become involved with people who treat us well. Once we stop overworking, overeating, and ignoring ourselves, then we'll choose to be surrounded by loving folks. We grow in love for ourselves and others.

As soon as I started putting into practice these suggestions, and began healing my heart and soothing my soul, I improved my situation.

One of the first things I had to do when learning how to heal my relationships was to figure out how to set boundaries that were right for me. At first, I wasn't even sure what a boundary was. I had to ask myself some important questions:

- Do I allow people to criticize and attack me?

- Do I view other people's opinions about me as more valid than my own opinions about myself?
- Do I put other people's needs above my own?
- Do I try to fix other people's lives, even if they don't ask me for help?
- Do I spend time with people who dismiss me when I say no and keep insisting I say yes?
- Do I overlook people's behavior and keep hoping they'll change?
- Do I believe that if only I figure out how to please people, they'll give me their approval and love?
- Do I minimize inappropriate behavior?

I answered all these questions with "Yes." I hadn't yet learned to love myself, so I kept staying in painful situations. I kept thinking that if only I figured it out, I would be able to reach these people; they would feel my love and love me in return. To give a twist to an old country-western song, I didn't have the sense to come in from the pain.

How could I set boundaries when I didn't know where I ended and other people began? I didn't really believe that when I said no, I had the right to ask other people to respect my answer. I felt that if someone needed me and seemed to have more difficulties than I had, then I should put all my energies into helping them, even if it meant neglecting myself.

A whole lot has changed since I began my journey toward self-love. There are several traps I can now avoid, and I've learned new ways to heal relationships. Here are several important concepts that go into healing relationships.

The If-Only Cycle

Until we truly love ourselves, we might become hooked in a cycle of addictive love. This happens when we're in love with people who don't love us unconditionally, and it occurs only when we don't love ourselves unconditionally.

Here's how it works: We find someone we must chase and convince to love us. They're stingy with their love and seem to always be on the verge of leaving us. We think that if only we do the right things to please them, they'll never abandon us. If only we make the right dinner, wear a sexier outfit, don't say that, and say this, they'll always love us. We please them and win their love for a while and feel high on their approval. But then they get angry (something always triggers them), and they withdraw. We're desperate to feel their love again, so we abandon our needs, our principles, and our self-esteem. We do whatever it takes to win them back, including forgetting ourselves completely. We're on edge and full of pain until we feel their love again. We're stuck in the if-only cycle.

We each have a responsibility to ourselves to fill our own wells. We can't become women of dignity and grace if we're totally focused on trying to please people and manipulate them into loving us and not abandoning us. When we stay in the fear that people will leave us (the problem), we can't see a way out (the solution). And we abandon ourselves every time. Self-abandoning is the opposite of self-loving.

We find people who don't love us unconditionally. We do something they think is wrong, and they withdraw their love. We're desperate to win them back, so we abandon ourselves to please them. They're pleased for a while, but then they withdraw their love. So we abandon ourselves again.

The more desperate we become, the more they withdraw. The following story illustrates this cycle.

Carolyn is a Columbia Law School graduate who had no problem standing up in a courtroom and prosecuting hardened criminals, but she cowered in front of her boyfriend. When she caught Ryan cheating on her, he promised he wouldn't do it again. So she gave him another chance. But he cheated on her again. Ryan got jealous if she talked to a colleague by the watercooler, yet he did whatever he wanted to do. If Carolyn complained, Ryan twisted around her comments and said that she was working so much that he needed some companionship. Or he told her it was a random fling and she was making a big deal about it. They reconciled. He told her he loved her, she felt immediate relief, and then he cheated again. And the cycle continued.

When Carolyn talked to me, she realized that she had to come out of her denial about Ryan's behavior. She was minimizing his dishonesty and disloyalty. She kept defending him and saying, "Maybe I should get a less high-pressure job, maybe I should spend more time with him ..."

We often stay in denial because we don't want to see what we don't want to see! If we're frightened to admit the truth, then it might take us a long time to admit to ourselves what's truly going on. Reality is sometimes so painful that we refuse to take it in. We try to gaslight ourselves and pretend something isn't happening because we wish it weren't happening.

That's awareness. This leads us to the next concept.

The Three *A*'s: Awareness, Acceptance, Action

When we become aware, we start to grow. Then we move toward acceptance. Carolyn needed to accept the idea that people's actions have to match their words.

Ryan told her that he wouldn't cheat on her again, and yet he kept doing it. His past behavior was a very good indicator of his future behavior. Even if Carolyn switched jobs or never left the house to spend more time with him, he would cheat unless he committed to changing himself, which he refused to do.

We eventually become aware of a situation, however painful it is. Then we accept it. It doesn't mean we like it. It only means that we accept that this is what's happening now. Finally, when we accept it, we realize we have choices. We have options. We can decide what we want to do about the situation. We have the right to take action!

Part of Carolyn's awareness meant connecting her present reality with her past experiences. Her father divorced her mother when Carolyn was in college. It dawned on her that she was petrified that Ryan would leave her the way her father had left her mother.

Carolyn was abandoning herself out of fear that Ryan would abandon her. Her fear of being left alone stopped her from seeing that he wasn't treating her the way she deserved to be treated. She kept ignoring herself and her needs because she was frightened that he'd leave her. But this is the truth: it doesn't matter who abandons us as long as we don't abandon ourselves.

I sat with Carolyn and spoke about how we teach people how to treat us. If we tolerate inappropriate behavior, then that's what we'll always get.

"Is the pain worth it?" I asked her.

Carolyn hesitated. "I don't know how to stop the cycle I'm in," she finally said. "It's definitely a loop."

I suggested that she make a list of what she was willing to accept and what she wasn't. What were the positive things she got out of the relationship? What were the negatives?

As she looked over the list, it dawned on her that the main reason she didn't want to break up with Ryan was the fear of being alone.

Yet instead of staying in the problem—which was her fear of being alone—we came up with some ideas for a solution. She made another list of things she could do after she broke up with him. It was a list of what she could do not only by herself but with herself and for herself. Here was her list:

- Write and say a vow of self-love and buy a ring
- See friends more
- Offer to babysit for friends with kids
- Go to the health club after work at least three times a week
- Sign up for free walking tours on the weekends
- Mentor a young woman in law school
- Maybe go on a dating app

- Do yoga
- Look in the mirror and tell myself that I won't let anyone mistreat me again

Carolyn also took another suggestion. When we hold a resentment about someone and can't stop thinking about them, we can give them a nickname. This allows us to detach a bit and puts a humorous spin on the situation. So every time she caught herself obsessing about Ryan, she called him "Why Him?" This put a smile on her face.

Carolyn broke up with Ryan a few days later and began planning the concrete things on her list, making a few small changes each day. She felt better almost overnight. Her fear of being alone no longer fueled her choices. By making the decision to love herself her priority, Carolyn was able to take action. She decided to stay celibate for six months to focus on herself. As she began to love herself more, she soon attracted someone who could love her in a healthy way. She healed her relationship by healing herself.

And it all began with self-love.

Self-Reflection

Is there a relationship that's robbing you of self-love? What can you do about it?

Learning to Argue

When I was growing up, I never saw my parents have an argument. They had screaming matches. Well, I should say that my mother yelled at my father, and my father walked out of the house. So I never learned how to deal with conflict. It always scared me (and still does).

Some women feel comfortable yelling at their partners; other women retreat. Some of us use sarcasm or turn bitter; others use the silent treatment. We learn most of our argument behaviors during childhood and from watching how our parents behaved.

The art of learning to love ourselves includes unlearning many things. We no longer need to repeat the behaviors from our childhood home. We can find new ways to behave, new ways to get angry, and new ways to express our fears.

Here are some tools that can help you navigate your way through the rough waters of disagreements.

Make Amends First

Pride often gets in the way of my making amends. "I'm not going to apologize to him first. He should apologize to me," I often say. I keep insisting that the other person should make the first move. Once again, I catch myself making rules that other people should follow. And really, do I want to be right or do I want to be happy?

The only rule to ending an argument is to end it as quickly as possible. What's the point of dragging it out? What's the benefit of stewing and blaming? That wastes our precious time on Earth and fills our minds and hearts with poison. There's no purpose in staying angry, unless it's to justify our self-righteousness and resentments.

The silent treatment is also a terrible form of punishment. I know women who use the silent treatment on their partners, former friends, and even children. My mother used to stop speaking to me for days. It was so hurtful. As I grew in self-love and trusted my perceptions more, I was able to laugh and say that she was playing the game called "Guess what I'm angry about." But it wasn't funny. I used to chase her and ask, "What did I do wrong this time?" Her silent treatment kept me her emotional prisoner. It kept me trapped.

So, I don't use the silent treatment. And I don't wait for the other person to apologize first. I can reach out and say something like, "I'm sorry for what's going on."

And what's so bad about being wrong, anyway? We can ask ourselves, "Do I want to be right, or do I want to be happy?"

Being the first to apologize pushes our pride to the side and focuses on the solution. We want to live in peaceful harmony with others.

Self-Reflection

What are the techniques you learned from your childhood home that you use in disagreements? What makes you the most uncomfortable in arguments? Do you scream? Do you use the silent treatment? Are you able to reach out and end an argument first? What new behaviors can you try?

The 1 Percent Rule

"When people bother you in any way, it is because their souls
are trying to get your divine attention and your blessing."
— Catherine Ponder

An important part of healing relationships is to accept our role in a problem. In every disagreement, I'm at the scene of the crime. I have a role to play. I've gone from thinking I was 100 percent right to admitting that maybe, just maybe, I might be only 99 percent right. Which means I'm still responsible for that other 1 percent, where I'm wrong. That 1 percent is our part in the solution.

We have to own up to that 1 percent. We still have to make amends for that 1 percent wrong, even if the other person was far wronger (I know that isn't a word!) than we were.

Self-Reflection

Are you willing to accept your 1 percent in a conflict?

Practice Listening

Part of learning how to heal our relationships is learning how to navigate disagreements. We learn how to listen, and we learn how to speak more effectively.

When we listen to just listen, not to respond, we're practicing acceptance. A woman said that she used to listen to a friend's story and then say, "Well, if you think that's bad, what I went through was worse." She said she was always competing with people and not really listening to their stories.

To listen is to practice being in the moment with someone. We're not thinking about what pearl of wisdom we can say, or how to change someone else's mind, or how our experience was worse or better. We're simply listening to their words. Actively listening. In fact, we're serving as witnesses.

Listening to others is a skill we learn once we've learned to listen to ourselves. When we're tuned in to ourselves, we can hear the beats and breaths and beauty of our hearts. With that skill, then, we can listen to others, but not to change them. We can simply hear them.

Relationships can fall apart into misunderstandings when one person says to the other, "You're not listening to me." We might hear the other person's words, but we're not truly listening.

One tool to practice to improve your listening skills is simply to repeat what the other person just said.

Let's say someone says to you, "I'm angry you didn't hug me when I was crying."

Maybe you were too upset to hug them. Yet you can reply, "You're angry. I hear that." By repeating what they said, you're honoring their feelings. Then you can ask, "What do you want me to do the next time?"

As I listen and am unsure how to respond to what someone is trying to tell me, I try to find the space between what I hear and how I respond. Taking a deep breath and pausing for the slightest moment saves me from getting into arguments, assuming the wrong thing, and deepening misunderstandings. I make sure that what I hear is really what's being said—and not just my fears or assumptions. This is challenging in real time, but it cools down a heated argument. We can say, "Is there another way you can say this so that I understand?" If we say it in this way, the other person feels that we want to understand them. It usually soothes an angry person and gets them to speak in a calmer manner.

Self-Reflection
How can you improve your art of listening?

Focusing on the Present and Focusing on Me
I no longer throw old arguments into a new one. When I'm in the middle of a conflict, I try to stay in the present and talk about what's bothering me *now*. I try to not keep score ("What you did, what you didn't do, what you should have done ...") I try to not repeat arguments from the past so I get lost in time. I try to no longer throw at my husband a mistake he made ten years ago. It's in the past. It's already passed.

One of the first things I learned was to not say to someone, "You always do this" or "You never do that." I stick to what just happened. I keep the focus not on what they did but on how I feel.

I try to not fly off the handle and scream. If I lose it, I lose it. If I'm angry, I try to take my anger out in appropriate ways: running to let off steam, hitting a pillow, or talking to someone else before I explode.

When my two sons were little, I was trying to teach this to them. "Try to start your sentence with *I*," I told my older son.

My younger son piped in, "Not *J* or *K*!"

I had to laugh. But I realize that if I start with how I feel, honestly sharing my experience, the other person doesn't feel attacked and can't argue back.

We can allow our words to simply exist in the air around us. We say them and release them. We listen to them and release them. We're healing our relationships simply by the way we speak and listen.

Self-Reflection

How can you improve the way you argue?

The Exit Sign

Sometimes, in the act of bringing more love into my life, I've been able to heal relationships. For example, I was holding on to a resentment about an old friend, and I reached out to her. I made amends for my 1 percent and tried to clear up the misunderstanding between us. She wasn't interested in hearing my apology or renewing our friendship. She was still angry at me and preferred to hold on to her anger. I realized that was her stuff. I'd done all I could, then walked toward the exit sign and left our friendship. I did so lovingly, but I had to let her go.

If people don't treat us appropriately—if they keep busting our boundaries or we feel more tolerated than celebrated—we'll know it's time to go. Like a bird that has to migrate, we don't have to stick around waiting for other people to love us. We love ourselves enough now to know that. We bless the people who were in our lives for a season, or a reason. We bless them for the lessons they taught us. We bless them and then release them and ourselves to continue our day full of self-love. Loving ourselves enough also means bidding people farewell.

Self-Reflection

Is there someone you need to make amends to? Is there a relationship you feel you need to let go of?

Afterword

I created *The Loving-Yourself Book* to guide you toward loving yourself. I wanted to share what I've learned on my own journey in the hope that it will help you.

I've learned that in the material world, when it comes to money, let's say, we like to save, if not hoard, our wealth in order to keep it. But in the spiritual world, the only way we get to keep our knowledge and even increase it is to give it away. So I wrote this book for you. I also wrote it for me. The tools and suggestions I've offered are those I continue to use. It was good for me to be reminded of them.

Yet there are some moments when my self-loving practice flies out the window. There are moments when I think that as much as I'm trying to love myself, I still feel pain and fear and discomfort. I even slip back into that place of self-hate and shame. I need to remember that I haven't stopped loving myself. The self-love is there, it's just more difficult to tap into. During a crisis or difficulty, I might lose sight of all the progress I've made.

The other day, for instance, a man shared a pornographic joke on a WhatsApp group I was in. I was livid; I lashed out as though I was a little girl fighting with all my might against that pediatrician.

I lost sight of the fact that I'm a grown woman and that man online won't hurt me. He might have made an inappropriate choice, but I could defend myself. I told him how wrong he was, and he apologized and didn't do it again. So maybe all that self-love I've been working toward gave me the strength to confront him. All the efforts I've made on behalf of myself allowed me to step out of denial and speak up. I would never have done that if I hadn't done all this work. Yay me! I counted it as a victory. In fact, I felt grateful for that man because his mistake showed me that I've changed. I'm no longer a helpless, hopeless little girl.

Sometimes we have to start from scratch all over again, making a fifteen-minute schedule to get through a new crisis, a new loss, a new challenge. Sometimes we feel lost and afraid; sometimes we lose our faith and feel overwhelmed. Those are times when we need to dig in and work harder at strengthening our connection with our Higher Power. Each difficulty is an opportunity to grow and become the women we're meant to become.

Here's the Self-Love Checklist that you answered at the beginning of the book. After reading this book and doing some (or most!) of the exercises, you now have the chance to answer them again. I hope you see a change in your answers. Even the tiniest change is progress. I encourage you to continue to use the tools in this book for a few months, and then answer the questions.

Self-Love Checklist

- Do you have a hidden fear that people won't like you when they find out who you really are?
- Do you secretly hate yourself?
- Do you live in a state of dissatisfaction with your life?
- Do you feel worthless?
- Do you find yourself always reacting to what other people say or do?
- Do you want to please people even at the risk of not pleasing yourself?
- Do you fear making decisions?
- Do you take care of other people's needs before you take care of your own?
- Do the people surrounding you disappoint you often?
- Do you need other people's approval?
- Do you feel hopeless?

And now, some questions that point you in a positive direction:

- Are you acting kinder to yourself?
- Are you practicing more self-care?
- Do you feel more self-esteem?
- Have you been able to let go of some of your expectations?

- Have you been able to nudge fear to the side and do what you want to do?
- Has your self-doubt decreased?
- Do you see a change in your decision-making?
- Are there areas in your life that you are able to accept more easily?
- Have you made any discoveries about your family history that impact your life?
- Have you taken steps to heal some of your relationships?
- Can you say you love yourself more today than you did yesterday?

It's important to remember that this is a daily practice. When I become impatient, I can remember that this isn't something I do one time and then I'm finished with it. It's a lifelong journey. I can be gentle with myself and recognize that every time I take the steps to love myself more, I am closer to happiness. I need to do the work each day by being good to myself; taking care of my heart, body, soul, and mind; accepting myself; and remembering that I'm doing the best I can. I want to keep evolving and growing, changing and moving forward.

I now love the woman I am, and I love you too. I hope this book helps you love yourself.

Resources

Books

Codependent No More: How to Stop Controlling Others and Start Caring for Yourself, Melody Beattie

The Gifts of Imperfection, Brené Brown

Rising Strong as a Spiritual Practice, Brené Brown

Love Warrior: A Memoir, Glennon Doyle

Untamed, Glennon Doyle

Self-Compassion: The Proven Power of Being Kind to Yourself, Kristin Neff

Set Boundaries, Find Peace: A Guide to Reclaiming Yourself, Nedra Glover Tawwab

The Year of Yes: How to Dance It Out, Stand in the Sun and Be Your Own Person, Shonda Rhimes

Self-help groups

www.Coda.org – Co-Dependents Anonymous, a support group for people who desire healthy and loving relationships

www.al-anon.org – Al-Anon Family Groups, a support group for people who are worried about someone else's drinking

www.oa.org – Overeaters Anonymous, a support group for people with compulsive eating and food behaviors

www.aa.org – Alcoholics Anonymous, a support group for people who have a problem with alcohol

www.adultchildren.org – Adult Children of Alcoholics, a support group for people who grew up in alcoholic homes

www.Wejoy.org – A variety of talks by Al-Anon and AA speakers, including Lorna K on meditation:
https://wejoy.org/php/speaker_detail.php?slug=lorna-k-2

About the Author

Diana Rachel Bletter is an award-winning writer and author of several books. She's an Ivy League graduate and accomplished journalist—and yet, having grown up in a highly-dysfunctional family full of alcoholism, narcissism, and depression, she felt worthless and full of self-hate.

At the untimely death of a dear friend, Diana made a vow not to spend the rest of her life hating herself, and embarked on a healing journey toward self-love. Since then, she has talked to countless women who struggle with self-hate. She now uses her own experience to help others transform their hurt into healing, triumph over their life challenges, and learn to love and celebrate the women they are.

To find out more about the author, visit:
www.dianabletter.com

Thank you for purchasing my book. I am happy to share that part of the proceeds goes to AMEN- The Land Where Women Heal, an organization for survivors of sexual violence. Thank you for supporting this cause with me.

I am extremely grateful that you invited me on your journey toward self-love and I hope you found value in these pages. Please share the book with your friends and family so that they, too, can learn the joys of loving themselves. And please, leave a review online. Your feedback is always appreciated and your support allows me to continue doing this important work—which is to help others love themselves more. So, pass on the love! Please go to https://mybook.to/TheLovingYourselfBook to leave a review.